generation
to
generation

other anthologies from
Sandra Haldeman Martz

Celebrating Aging
When I Am an Old Woman I Shall Wear Purple
If I Had My Life to Live Over I Would Pick More Daisies
Grow Old Along with Me—The Best Is Yet to Be
*The Tie That Binds: A Collection of Writings about Fathers & Daughters /
     Mothers & Sons*

Celebrating Women's Lives
I Am Becoming the Woman I've Wanted
If I Had a Hammer: Women's Work in Poetry, Fiction, and Photographs

Family Humor
There's No Place Like Home for the Holidays

Also edited by Sandra Haldeman Martz, with images by Deidre Scherer
Threads of Experience

generation
to
generation

edited by
sandra martz and
shirley coe

Papier-Mache Press
Watsonville, CA

02 01 00 99 98   10 9 8 7 6 5 4 3 2 1

ISBN: 1-57601-072-4 Softcover

Design and composition by Elysium Design
Editors' photograph by Thomas Burke
Copyediting by Shirley Coe
Proofreading by Cathey Cordes
Manufactured by Malloy Lithographing, Inc.

Library of Congress Cataloging-in-Publication Data

    Generation to Generation / edited by Sandra Martz and Shirley Coe.
        p.   cm.
    ISBN 1-57601-072-4 (pbk. alk. paper)
        1. Intergenerational relations—Literary collections. 2. American literature—
    20th century. I. Martz, Sandra. II. Coe, Shirley. 1956–
    PS509.I57G46   1998
    810.8'0355—dc21   98-5395
                                                       CIP

⊕ This book is printed on acid-free, recycled paper containing a minimum of
  85 percent total recycled fiber with 15 percent postconsumer de-inked fiber.

For the children we once were
and
the old women we'll someday be.

contents

preface

Whether family, friends, or brief acquaintances, our lives are enriched by our connections with people older and younger than ourselves. All it takes is time and an opportunity to get to know one another. Of these relationships, the bond between grandparents and grandchildren is one of the most important and most enduring. Grandparents are the keepers of our heritage; grandchildren are the forgers of our future. As children, our grandparents often provided our first experience of unconditional love. If we lived in the same community, we shared common interests and made important contributions to each other's knowledge, awareness, and self-perception.

Over the last several decades, however, it has grown increasingly difficult to establish and maintain the extended family relationships that characterized and sustained communities in earlier times. Today grandparents may live in adults-only retirement communities, grown sons and daughters pursue careers in distant towns, and teenagers cloister themselves apart from the family. We attempt to bridge the growing generation gaps and strengthen our family ties with family visits, reunions, electronic mail, and old-fashioned letter writing.

While working to maintain our long-distance relationships, however, we don't want to overlook the at-hand opportunities to forge new friendships with older and younger people. The people we meet every day—neighbors, teachers, students, volunteers, coworkers—are potential new friends and companions.

Generation to Generation pays homage to these possibilities. Moving chronologically from the various narrator's perspectives, these stories, poems, and photographs explore the richness and diversity of intergenerational relationships, both within and outside our families.

Addressing childhood issues, the writers explore how care and attention from adults can help children develop a strong sense of self. In "Possibilities," a granddaughter and her newly widowed grandmother jointly explore a future without limits: *"Sing with me, Emogene; singing frees the spirit,"* encourages Grandma Turner. In "Jackie West," an older neighbor nurtures a ten-year-old girl after school with warm meals and healing words to contradict the racism she encounters from classmates.

In the stories of free-spirited older men and women, we see the power of countering stereotypes of what it means to be older. When "Aunt Hattie Visits" unexpectedly from Florida to shop for a bright new party dress, her niece finds it impossible to resist her aunt's exuberance for life. *Aunt Hattie's theory is that I think too much. "Comes from reading all those books," she says. "Sometimes you just have to feel something and do it."* Inspiring his neighbors with his physical agility, "The Oldest Man in the World" is *old, old, howling old, perishing old / But can still turn a somersault and will / If the request is from someone he knows well.*

Many readers will recognize the opportunity to focus outside one's self that comes with being in a support role for others. The free-wheeling cab driver in "The Hundred-Dollar Tip" initially assumes his "weekly" is just another fare—*some kind of big-shot business man*—but soon establishes a meaningful connection with his elderly rider that changes his perspective on life. In "Soup for Victoria," a well-intentioned but somewhat beleaguered young woman learns that true friendship with an older family friend requires being able to receive as graciously as she is prepared to give.

Several stories address the poignant bond between the very old and the very young as they deal with isolatation. In "The Tea Party," an older woman resists her daughter's urgings to move to a retirement home; instead she reaches back to her own childhood memories to re-create a celebration for the little girl who's just moved in next door. A tender bond is formed between a speech-impaired grandfather and his beautiful, silent, autistic granddaughter in "The Swing." Only with each other do they both feel truly heard.

We've been deeply touched by the intimacy and sharing of these lives. We hope *Generation to Generation* will inspire you to reflect on the joys of your own past intergenerational relationships and look forward to those that await you in the future.

—Sandra Martz and Shirley Coe

generation
to
generation

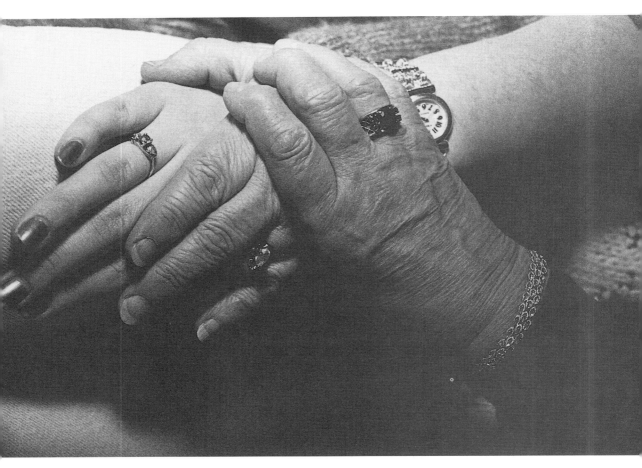

Photo by Alexandra Buxbaum

over my shoulder
Ruth Daigon

Don't look back. Something might be gaining on you.
—Satchel Paige

As I flip backward through the album
the family is young and growing younger.
Background foliage, almost real,
frames cross-eyed cousins innocent
of spinsterhood, aunties free of pregnancies,

my mother with healthy heart and no
regrets, her oldest son still focused, her
younger's slanted smile. Here, my father's
amputated finger strums his mandolin.

One slim sister half-turns to her husband
erasing all the silent years ahead.
The other leans a smooth cheek
up against the shadow of an arm.

And I'm still wearing tap shoes and my
tightrope-walker's smile. Only my bearded
grandfather dies inward like a tree while
grandmother shifts slowly through the album.

Uncle Dave's nineteen again before the current
drags him down. All of us, warm and urgent
unaware of empty places waiting to be filled
by negatives yet to be developed.

possibilities
Judith Bell

"Emogene!" Grandmother Turner called from downstairs.

In one motion Emogene rolled out of bed, grabbed her clothes, and ran for
the door. From the safe distance of the hall she looked back at the attic. The
clothes of those relatives most recently dead hung near the open doorway; her
grandfather's overalls were right up front. "Suits the pigs and cows," she could
remember him saying on his way to or from the fields and barns. Houses made
him almost as uncomfortable as idleness and pleasure. He had seen to it that
in his house there was little of either.

She tried to imagine the bright print dresses Grandmother Turner now favored
crowded in next to his faded overalls, but the flounce of their full skirts refused
to be reined in with the dead. The openness of the attic reminded her of the
Indian burials she had seen in Westerns where the dead were put up on stilts
and left right out among the living.

She pulled on her shorts and top and with her sandals in one hand, tiptoed
quietly down the hall. She stopped at the last door before the stairs, turned
the knob slowly, easing it past its squeak. She wove her way through a jumble
of steamer trunks, gilded picture frames, bureaus, and wardrobes. Here Grandmother Turner kept all the things that had been left to her that would fit nowhere
else. Reaching the center of the room Emogene stopped, taking in the papery
decay that was all around her. Undisturbed dust accumulated, wood rotted,
bookbindings warped, pages turned yellow and brittle, tearing as easily as fall
leaves.

"Emogene, you awake?" Grandmother Turner called again. "Get down here
and eat your breakfast. We have to get to the beauty parlor." Emogene ran
lightly over to the door, stuck her head into the hall, and called, *"Coming."*
Slipping on her sandals she turned to take in the room once more before
running downstairs.

"You move slower than any twelve-year-old I ever saw." Grandmother Turner shoved cereal boxes toward Emogene's place at the table, gathered her pocket-book and keys. "Get on over here and eat something. I can't be late for my hair tint."

In the six months since Granddaddy died, Grandmother had given up two things: cooking and staying home. She was in the full glory of what she called her retirement. All the relatives she had waited on for forty years were finally dead, and she'd taken to pleasuring herself with a vengeance. Emogene had spent every weekend since her grandfather's death with her grandmother. Saturday mornings they went to the beauty parlor, had lunch at the drugstore. Sunday mornings they went to church.

At first, Emogene's mother had come too. But she claimed that "carting Mama all over the face of the earth" wore her out, and Grandmother decided that just because her husband had never let her learn to drive was no reason not to now. After a few Saturday mornings of practice in the church parking lot with her daughter, Grandmother sent Emogene's mother home, insisting she have Emogene each weekend for company.

"Do you think I need a new permanent wave, Emogene? My hair's not curling like it was." Grandmother Turner bent down to pour milk on Emogene's cereal, stared at her reflection in the toaster. "I could never get it today, that Ruby keeps herself booked up tight as a nut. Maybe I'll get me a new hat instead." Arms folded across the low shelf of her bosom, she watched Emogene spoon up her cereal. "Eat a little more then come on out here to the piano," she said, moving into the hall. "Let's us play a hymn before we leave."

Emogene dropped her spoon and was on her grandmother's heels, following her into the dim hallway that ran the length of the house. Grandmother Turner played with a sense of purpose. With the strike of each chord, the force of her intentions coursed through the knotted veins that rose and fell along the backs of her hands.

"Sing with me, Emogene; singing frees the spirit." She played the opening bars of her favorite hymn. Emogene's voice was lost in the fullness of her grandmother's as they sang: "Shall we gather at the river, the beautiful, beautiful river? Shall we gather at the river where bright angel's feet have trod?"

As long as Emogene could remember, Grandmother Turner had spent all her free moments at the piano. In the middle of making biscuits or a pie, she would wipe her hands across the front of her apron and run into the hall to play one more hymn before Granddaddy came in from the fields.

"Leave off playing that thing," he would bellow before he was halfway in the back door. "Is that what you do all day while I'm out working?" After his mother died he was never sure what his wife had been up to and this worried him. He would go straight to the dining room table and sit, the strain of being indoors wearing on him while he waited for his supper to appear. Her lips gone tight, the color pressed out of them, Grandmother Turner would close the cover over the keys and rise to return to the kitchen.

Emogene remembered the day Granddaddy's hold on her grandmother came to an end. The afternoon after his burial, Emogene sat with her grandmother in the parlor amid the maze of heavy Victorian furniture, the shades drawn against the cold air seeping through the glass. Empty of mourners for the first time in days, the house was quiet. On the mantle, tiny porcelain men and women—the corners chipped off coats and dress tails, turned this way and that, bowing and curtsying to one another—waited endlessly for the dance to begin. Beside them a grandmother clock ticked to the tock of the grandfather clock in the corner. There was only the sound of their forks hitting their plates as they finished off the last of a lemon chiffon cake. A howling wind rushed down the chimney, swept through the house, slammed doors in its wake.

"That was the Holy Ghost." Grandmother Turner pressed her finger against her plate to get the last of the cake crumbs. A clear sign that she had had enough of this mourning business, she got up and went in to her piano.

"That ought to do us for hymn singing this morning." Grandmother Turner closed the cover over the keys. "Go on out and get the car windows rolled down, Emogene."

Emogene opened the windows all the way; Grandmother Turner wouldn't mind the wind since they were going to the beauty parlor first thing. She left the doors open to let the seat covers cool off. She rocked back on her heels, waiting.

Grandmother Turner liked to take the back stairs one at a time, holding the banister for good measure. "I'll not break my hip rushing; only trip I'll have then will be to the hospital."

"I want to eat at Walgreen's when we get done at the beauty parlor," Emogene said once Grandmother Turner was on solid ground.

"Suits me fine." Grandmother Turner motioned for her to get in the car. "I wouldn't mind having me a cold plate, hot as it's going to be out today."

Ruby's Beauty Bungalow was in an old Esso Station on the main road leading into town. Not one for parallel parking, Grandmother Turner favored Ruby's and her big parking lot over the beauty parlor in town. She usually gave Emogene a dollar and sent her across the road to Craven's Store for Sugar Daddys and fireballs—candy hard enough to last through their morning at Ruby's—but today they were running late.

"Get on in there and tell Ruby I'm here; she might give away my appointment," Grandmother Turner said before she had the car stopped. "Besides, I want to put on some lipstick before I make a public appearance."

Inside Ruby's the chemical smells of dye and permanent waving fluid overrode the perfume of shampoos and rinses. Hairdryers roared above the hiss of Spraynet cans and the hum of women talking. Emogene wandered past the beauty operators to where Ruby settled a customer under the hairdryer.

"Now, Ruby, careful with that heat," the woman was saying. "I get a headache something awful when the ear pieces on my glasses heat up."

Ruby clucked sympathetically, turned the heat on high.

"Well, Emogene, is it you here for the works today?" Ruby patted her blond beehive, turning to give herself an admiring smile in the mirrored wall above the hairdryer.

"No ma'am. My grandmother says to tell you she'll be right in."

"All right, honey." Ruby leaned over the coffee table where she kept her magazines. "Here's some picture books to keep you occupied."

Emogene held the magazines close, followed Ruby over to the chair across from her station. She sifted through the magazines, discarding the *Ladies' Home Journal.* The fashion magazines were Emogene's favorite part of her Saturday mornings here. Somewhere inside them was the secret to a different life. She could feel it move just beyond her fingertips when she turned the glossy, rich-colored pages.

Grandmother Turner walked in the door. "Ruby, I want you to go easy on the blue in this hair tint."

"You're the one had your mind set on blue." Ruby snapped the pink plastic cape sharply in the air. "Let's go back and get you rinsed out." Ruby patted Emogene's knee. "We'll be right back."

Emogene hardly noticed. She was already lost in her magazine where tall graceful women wore elegant clothes in exotic places. Here they were in Egypt by the pyramids, looking cool as ice in long, flowing robes, the desert sun making their faces shine like gold. "Let's go to Egypt sometime," she said as her grandmother settled into Ruby's chair.

"Egypt, huh?" Grandmother Turner paused, watching Emogene in Ruby's big mirror. "Careful you don't tell your mama about that. She'll be on me again for feeding you big ideas. Let me see what you're looking at."

Emogene leaned forward, holding the magazine close to her grandmother's face.

"Those gals'll be burnt to a crisp wearing such as that in the desert. Maybe we will go to Egypt. Catch me some rich sheik, right, Ruby?"

"What you want some sheik bossing you around for, Miz Turner?" Ruby shook her head as she combed blue dye through Grandmother Turner's hair.

Grandmother Turner sniffed. "I don't suppose they're any worse than men anywhere else."

"Well, I hate to be the one reminding you," Ruby began, although Emogene could see she didn't mind at all, "but to hear you tell it, you already had one man too many telling you what to do."

Grandmother Turner's mouth went all tight. In her mind Emogene saw her grandmother close the piano, go in the kitchen to wait on Granddaddy. "No ma'am, I won't be going to Egypt," she said firmly. The old look was gone as suddenly as it came. Winking at Ruby she said, "I'll stay right here where the men with sense know who's boss, right, Ruby?" The women roared, Ruby holding onto Grandmother Turner's arm to keep from falling down.

"Well, Emogene." Ruby leaned into the mirror, dabbed her tearing eyes with her little finger. "Maybe we better give you some curls for your big trip."

"You'll never get a curl to hold on that stringy head," Grandmother Turner said.

"We'll see about that." Ruby wet Emogene's hair down with setting lotion, twisted it into tight pin curls, and deposited her under the hairdryer. "Helen," she called to the idle manicurist, "Miss Emogene is fixing to leave for Egypt."

Helen hurried over with two bottles of pink polish. "How about one of these, doll baby?"

Emogene pointed to the bottle that glowed like the caftan one of the women wore in the magazine. She sat turning the pages with her fingertips, watching the fluorescent light catch the colors in her polish.

She closed her eyes, surrendered to the roar and heat of the dryer. She found herself in Egypt, surrounded by white sand, her nails lit by a desert moon. Off in the distance the sharp wind whipped the sheik's robes about him.

Emogene began to hum a hymn.

infinity
Amber Coverdale Sumrall

The idea of infinity makes me crazy
I tell my grandmother
after Uncle Eugene dies,
his soul spirited away
like smoke on the Santa Ana winds.
She leads me to her dressing table:
a shrine of crystal candleholders,
silver urns and music boxes.
She lights candles
arranges the half-circle of mirrors
tells me to look into the glass.
This is infinity, she says.

In the shimmer of shadow and light
I gaze at reflection after reflection,
watch myself shrink
until I nearly vanish.
Time shifts like a dream
rolling slowly out of control.

whisper garden
Susan Kan

Mrs. B. squats in her garden until her knees give out. She lifts her wide, cotton skirt to sit flat in the aisles, the dark soil pressing into the backs of her thighs. It is an early hot day in May. One sleeve slides off her shoulder as she lifts the small basil plants, the tiny spindling arms of the tomatoes, and pushes them into the holes she cups out with her other hand.

She checks on her seedlings before sunrise when dew clings to the grass in miniature lobes of light. She goes out in her flip-flops and nightgown, feels for them on moonless nights. On her hands and knees, she crawls between the rows. Once she lay down, smiling queerly to herself that this would help keep the weeds back.

When the moon is high, she measures the shadows that pepper and broccoli shoots make. Her fingers play with the light underneath the tender leaves, tickling. Dark lines cap her fingernails.

Mrs. B. runs outside when lightning strikes close. She touches snakes with her bare feet. She walks along cliffs but takes stairs one at a time. She is quiet and fierce in her eyes. She never brushes and her teeth are hard.

She whispers into holes like a lover does, then plants herself. The mysteries of her veins and muscles meet and connect under the cover of her skin. Mrs. B. hums in her garden. Her garden is a queen-sized bed.

Meg peeks between the slats of the picket fence. Mrs. B. wears a silver necklace. Meg follows the thick chain down to its teardrop stone, the color of ash, but pretty. The pendant swings with Mrs. B.'s breasts when she leans over the basil to whisper to the lettuce, and it knocks against the leaves like a playmate.

She waves to Meg. Meg lifts her hand in a reluctant salute. Come, child, Mrs. B. says. Her mouth is a spider on her face, wrinkled legs reaching in.

Meg watches Mrs. B. whisper secrets into holes before planting. She leans over, her breasts brushing against the ground, her mouth inches from the place where the pepper plant will go; her nose fills with dry soil. Whispering this way, no one can hear.

Mrs. B. cuts her own tangled hair, brown, turning grey, and robins take it away. Her body is full as a fancy couch and pleasing. Her hands are large and working, can carry children and worries together in balance. Her feet are flat and sure.

Meg squeezes through the pickets until the wood shines smooth as fast water. Mrs. B. says she loves the land first, animals second, children third. Together, they rescue sparrows fallen from nests.

Meg pokes the earth with a dry stick. What were you saying to the ground? she asks. I saw you.

Mrs. B. fills a peck basket with zucchini, holds two red tomatoes in her palms every day of August. She pulls carrots, big as swords, boasting orange. She cuts red cabbage, heavy as water, creased and veined. Mrs. B. lies in the grass next to her garden when the sun slant is a roof line, and she eats red peppers like apples, the crunch sweet and hollow at the same time.

Meals and meals, Mrs. B. eats vegetables raw and unwashed, laced with her whispers. They nourish her, sustain her, but leave her always wanting more.

Here is the story, she says one day, sitting on the grass. She looks straight up through the poplar leaves, and Meg does the same. With her eyes still on the sky, Mrs. B. says, This story happened long ago, before the wind told the wishes of these trees. Then she begins: Apollo turned King Midas's ears into the ears of an ass.

You mean a donkey?

Apollo said he was giving the ears a more appropriate shape since the king was so dull and stupid. Midas hid them under a cap especially made for hiding, but the barber who cut his hair saw them. He was the only one who saw them. He promised never to tell, but the secret was a burden on him so that finally he went way out to a distant field, as far as he could walk. There, he dug a hole as long as his legs, and he was a tall man. He knelt down close and spoke soft as air into it. He whispered into the hole, "The king has asses' ears."

Donkeys', Meg says.

He felt relieved and filled the hole up so that no one could tell it'd been dug. But in the springtime, long grass grew up there. And then the wind blew, and when the wind blew, you could hear, blowing in the breeze, "The king has asses' ears, the king has asses' ears." Mrs. B. whispers those buried words so that Meg has to lean closer to hear. Mrs. B.'s hot breath touches Meg's arm.

Okay, says Meg sitting up only to bend her little body again, like a sprout in rain. She listens to the beans, down against the leaves. A bug crawls up her hair like Jack and the stalk.

Mrs. B. leans into the ground with her. Who you whisper your secrets to, that's who you feel closest to.

Tell me some secrets that you planted.

Mrs. B.'s voice is deep and smooth, like beer. When she speaks, the sound comes not from her mouth but from her stomach and rolls up her throat like a heavy ball across the sky. Not loud, but thorough and deliberate.

I say, I am a fish against concrete, gasping for water. I am a dancer without music. She lifts a handful of dirt and makes a black snowstorm fall. I am snowplowing down a steep slope.

It sounds like magic, but so sad.

I am not superstitious, she shakes her cheeks at Meg. Supercilious maybe. Then she whispers into the soil again.

Yes, Meg says, super.

Mrs. B. wears a barrette on top of her head that holds a hairy wave. It was engraved so long ago that the picture is a shadow. Mrs. B. says, sparrows flying. Meg says, picket fence.

Meg brings Mrs. B. books with pictures. They listen to the winds play the grass. Mrs. B. hears things. She keeps a notebook, but the handwriting is indecipherable.

Photo by Marilyn Nolt

12

chewing thread
Patricia Garfinkel

Grandmother made all my clothes,
basting them on me as I turned
slowly through miles of twirling skirts.

While I spun in place, she made me
chew a strand of thread to distract
the Devil, warning that to stitch

on someone brings bad luck.
I would move a small lump of thread
and spittle across my tongue,

grinding every color in the thread basket
against her fear. Red and green
for winter wools, pale yellow

and pink for ballet skirts, magenta
and navy for corduroy pants. I outgrew
the clothes before their colors dimmed,

but the lasso of her superstition holds
me now to chew those threads into rope
to catch a devil of my own making.

jackie west
Lisa Vice

When I was a child, we lived for a year on a dead-end road outside Meddybemps, Maine. My mother was a counselor at the family planning clinic in Machias where she tried to convince young girls not to do what she'd done. She'd been what was called—with a great deal of shame attached because it was more hidden then—an unwed teenage mother.

She started out at the clinic a few years before as the cleaning girl, going in weekends to yank the vacuum around and mop while I sat in the waiting room coloring or flipping through glossy magazines, falling asleep on the sofa, my cheek stuck to the vinyl cushions. Later, after she got her high school diploma, she nearly ran the clinic. But it didn't pay enough.

Before we moved to Meddybemps, we'd been living in a log cabin on the dump road, a place so dark that in May, snow still lingered in the woods at the edge of the cabin and blackflies thick as smoke surrounded us the minute we set foot outdoors. Our new house was rent free, in exchange for our presence there at the top of the hill. Use the money you save on rent to buy a decent wood-stove, John Nelson, the man whose house it was told my mother. But she didn't. I remember her fussing with the cast-iron box stove, cursing. When she stoked the fire, the room would fill with smoke and sometimes, at dawn, all the logs she'd put on before bed would catch at once, and I would wake up to the sound of the stove rumbling like an old train clattering by.

The house looked like a chicken coop. A cedar-shingled shed-roofed construction with three rooms, each slightly larger than a double bed. There was a hand pump in the kitchen, an improvement for us—the log cabin had no plumbing at all, and what water we'd needed we had lugged home from Stimpson's Springs, the water sloshing over the floor of the car as we bumped over the washboard road. This new house had electricity too—a luxury after the cabin's kerosene lamps.

John Nelson had tried to make a go of it as a strawberry farmer and before he left, he plowed his strawberry plants into the dirt. He said he didn't want folks coming up there picking over them, taking whatever they wanted. When I think of this place, the memory is always accompanied by the smell of strawberries rotting in the hot sun and the calls of crows swooping down to eat their fill.

"It's a step up," my mother said, as she always did, each time we moved. "It always gets a little better," she said as she unpacked our boxes and swept the rough wood planks. We had moved already eight times—I was only seven—and would move again ten more times before settling finally in New York City where I live now. After I graduated from high school, my mother went back to Maine. Though she tried, she never really belonged in the city. She was like a wildflower you pull up out of the woods and try to grow in a flowerpot. She only moved to the city for me. By then, I was used to her refrain: "It's a step up." But I never got used to moving. The packing and unpacking. The sorting. "Can you live without this?" The boxes filled and emptied. The little things you do to make a home. Often I dream everything I own is in boxes stacked around my bed. I wake up filled with panic and have to turn on the light to reassure myself I'm home, in the apartment where I live now. A place I hope never to leave. But back then, I was at the mercy of my mother, as all children are.

Out behind John Nelson's house was a farm pond. Sometimes in the evenings my mother and I would stand in the tall grass listening to the frogs croak, mosquitoes hovering around us as the moon rose, and I would pull her arm across me, push my nose into the damp wool sleeve of her sweater. When I think of her now, there is always the taste of that wool against my teeth.

There were no other children out on that dead-end road, but it was just as well. I didn't make friends easily. I was too different. With my brown skin. My dark curly hair. The children at school were all ruddy faced and pale headed, and I felt as alien as I was.

One day after school, instead of waiting in the house for my mother to come home from work—she had decided I was old enough to be left on my own—I ran down the hill as fast as I could and there at the bottom was Jackie West, staring up the road at nothing in particular, sitting on a stained and weather-scarred easy chair on a cement slab in front of her house. Her yard was littered with car parts: chrome bumpers, twisted steering wheels, a winch hooked to a rusted engine dangling from a heavy chain, and more stray cats than she could keep track of prowling through the weeds. From that day on, I ran down the hill as soon as the school bus dropped me off. Jackie was my first friend and the only company I had that year as I waited for my mother to chug up the hill, sparks flying out the tailpipe of her car.

It was Jackie I finally asked. I had come close to asking my mother in the evenings when she heated water for my bath or in the mornings as I got ready for school when it was still dark and she would be at the stove stirring oatmeal. But then she would turn to brush the snow from the floor where it had sifted in around the edges of the window. Or I would watch her get down on her back to wrap more insulation around the water pipe, terrified it would freeze, and I could never ask.

Sometimes I longed to comfort her but had no idea how. My mother grew very thin that year. Even the skin on her face seemed thin, with a sheen to it like waxed paper. And though she was young, her brown hair was streaked with white. She would smile and hang up the pictures I drew. She would kiss me good night and let me wrap my arms around her neck before she tucked me under the thick sleeping bag, worrying I would be cold. She would giggle at the riddles I told. But there was always a sadness I couldn't touch. Sometimes now I think how like sisters we were, two little girls feeling alone in the night, growing up together.

When I look back, it's hard for me to believe just how in the dark I was. But how was I supposed to understand? Sure. We live in an age of technology. Men landed on the moon the day I was born. The global village and all that. But we had no TV. And though Jackie did, it had no sound, only a fuzzy picture always threatening to flicker out.

The way I figure it, Jackie West was the closest thing to a father I will ever have, and I think she'd be proud to hear me say so. But it did make my mother nervous, I think, for me to spend time with this large woman in steel-toed boots whose hands were stained with car grease. Whose house was in worse shape than ours. My mother told me to stay home after school, but after a while she expected me to be at Jackie's and would toot on her way home and wait for me to run across the path of her headlights, my rubber boots slapping the icy road, my shadow long and looming before I jumped into the car beside her and helped her scrape away the ice her breath had made on the windshield.

I hope she's not any trouble, my mother would say to Jackie. Once she tried to give her money, but Jackie just stuffed her hands deeper into her pockets saying, "She's no trouble. No trouble at all. Don't you worry about it none. She's a fine girl."

One day my mother didn't come home when we expected her. We learned later she'd had a flat tire and was stuck on the side of the road in the dark, the lugs frozen on so tight she couldn't loosen them even though she stood on the tire iron the way she'd learned to, giving it all her weight. So Jackie made me supper, cooking steak in a beat-up fire-blackened aluminum pan. I had never eaten meat before. My mother was a vegetarian. Not so much for philosophical reasons or for the health of it. Meat was something she could do without and save a few pennies. I would go to school with rice cakes spread with peanut butter. Prunes wrapped in wax paper. Carrot sticks in a damp paper towel. What's that? the children would ask as they bit into their baloney sandwiches, their fingers clutching the spongy white bread spread with bright yellow mustard. They would laugh and point at my food as the crumbs from their chocolate cookies spilled down their chests.

I remember Jackie cooking that steak for me, how the flames leapt into the pan, and how she squirted the fire with a spray bottle of water she kept by the stove. One of the things I liked best about Jackie West was the fact that she had only a thumb and pinkie finger on her right hand. With the other fingers gone, that part of her hand looked like the sole of a foot. But she managed okay. Every time I asked, she would tell a different story of what had happened to her hand: caught in a window fan when she was a kid; the ax slipped when she was chopping wood; a she-bear crept out of the bushes and ate her fingers one-two-three. Sharks and buzzards and train wheels. Frostbite and boiling grease and mad dogs. "I'm no stranger to pain," she would say and grin her lopsided grin. Now, when I think of it, when I picture Jackie's hand, I see the smooth flesh where knuckles should have been and I realize there are no scars and imagine she was born this way, one hand like a claw.

Jackie West served me my first steak, heavily doused with Tabasco sauce and I ate it like I'd been eating it my whole life, cutting into the red meat, chewing the gristly fat. After that, she took to sharing her supper with me every day, starting to cook soon after I arrived. We ate hamburgers on grease-soaked buns, pork chops with crispy fat edges, sausages that sputtered in that pan. She would pull brownies from the oven, and they were so hot we had to blow on the sticky chocolate before we could bite into them. We ate ice cream out of the carton, digging in with our bent spoons, fighting each other for the nuts. Later at home, I would pick at my mother's meals, pretending to eat the sticky brown rice, to chew the slippery, translucent cabbage. I'd mash the beans with my fork, but really I was just moving the food around on my plate. I let her worry over me, never confessing what I'd already eaten.

I remember the day I asked Jackie what was on my mind. It was one of those January days when the sun starts to set at three o'clock and the air smells of snow and the wind makes your cheeks burn when you step into a heated room. We both kept our coats on in Jackie's house; it was that cold even though she had her stove stoked with wood. Jackie was tinkering with a fishing reel, telling me come spring, we would catch a mess of togue, and I just out and asked her. I have to remind myself sometimes just how stranded out there I was, with no idea about much of how I came to look the way I did. Now I am twenty-six years old. Older than my mother was then. I ride the subway to work. I walk down the avenues. I don't stand out in the crowd. There are people like me everywhere I turn. But then, in that town, in the schoolhouse of fifty children, I was a novelty even to myself.

"What's a nigger?" I asked, watching Jackie's good hand hold a screwdriver poised above the reel.

"Come again?" Jackie had a tiny silver screw pinched in the corner of her mouth; her long, thick hair was tucked down the back of the flannel shirt she'd pulled on over her sweater.

"What's a nigger?" I asked again, hoping it had nothing to do with sex. I assumed I knew everything there was about that subject what with the books and pamphlets my mother brought home, figuring, I guess, that if I was informed I could make a choice. Not do what she did. All I knew about this was she ran away from home and came back with me. It was the sixties, she once said, as if that explained everything.

When I think about that day at Jackie's, I can still picture my red shoes, the scuffed leather toes worn down to grey and my brown legs sticking out from the ends of my pants, my yellow socks drooping over the tops of my shoes like loose skin.

"Where'd you hear that?" Jackie asked, scraping back her chair.

"School."

"Huh," she said. "Huh." She got up slowly and reached for something on top of the refrigerator. "Look what I got us," she said and tore the cellophane open with her teeth and shook several cookies onto my lap. They were my favorites. Pink marshmallow with flecks of coconut on top. I ate one, licking off the coconut first, then biting into the marshmallow, eating it down to the cookie underneath.

"It's something special," Jackie said. "Special as these here cookies. You better believe it."

And I did believe it as I sat on the sprung sofa, a cat curled on either side of me purring, steaks sizzling on the stove. I believe it still and think of Jackie when my boyfriends—they are always dark-skinned men who don't stay long enough for the real love to begin—ask why it is I act so white.

The day we said good-bye, Jackie West offered me her good hand to shake. We were moving this time to Bangor. To an apartment with central heat, and my mother was going to college.

"It's got a flush," I told Jackie. "And a real bathtub."

"Put her here, tiger," she said, clasping my hand hard. Her palm was lined with black grease, red and rough and cold.

That was the last time I saw Jackie West. She was sitting in her chair by the front door staring ahead at nothing in particular just like she'd been sitting that day I ran down the hill out of breath into her life.

Photo by Marianne Gontarz

crayon, 1955
Susan Vreeland

One summer, when the raspberries along Miss Haskin's fence hung down all ripe and ready and I didn't know what to do with dolls anymore, Gramp came to our house to die. That meant I had to move out of my bedroom and set up camp near the living room sofa the day he moved in, the same day Miss Haskin, our neighbor, asked me to water her plants.

We had just moved and, without friends yet, I stayed at home, played "Doggie in the Window" on my record player about fifty times a day, and waited for fourth grade to start. "Go in, talk to Gramp," Mom said, but I hardly knew what to say. He was so old he seemed like someone from another country. I pretended to find something to do on the back deck, drawing or embroidery or a book, but my things were hard to get to. Daddy had set up Gramp's easel right next to the bed and a table for his brushes and paints. I felt cramped with his things on top of mine. I didn't want to look at him lying there in my bed in his stringy old man's robe the color of raw chicken liver. But he was watching me so I had to say something.

"I have a job," I said. He raised his eyebrows, kind of like he was glad I'd talked to him. "Taking care of Miss Haskin's plants."

"Who's that?"

"Just the grey old maid next door. She walks like a flamingo. Honest. She plops her big feet down and then her knees bend and jerk like creaky hinges, and she has a cube for a head."

"Jenny!"

"It's true. Her mouth's too big, and her eyeballs are in scooped-out holes, and she blinks a lot, but other than that, she's okay."

Gramp's mouth tried to smile. "Jenny, Jenny, look a little deeper," he said.

What was I missing? Once Mom called her an *intellectual*. She made it sound bad, but I'd always been told that being smart was a good thing. I felt sorry Miss Haskin had to live alone, and wondered what she did with her life.

"She's going on vacation," I said to Gramp. "But not a normal trip, like to the Grand Canyon or Yosemite. She's going to Guatemala, just to stay in one place and dig. Something called arc——."

"Archeology."

"Is that like a search for buried treasure?"

"Sort of."

The day after Miss Haskin left, I marched out to the sidewalk, her key on a rubber band on my wrist. I turned left into her driveway and flapped my feet down toes last, lifting my knees high like she did, then looked back at our bay window. Mom would give me a talking-to if she caught on. I opened the door into a dark entryway. It smelled cool. Once my eyes worked right, I could see it was our house, only flip-flopped. Where we turned right to go down the hall, Miss Haskin turned left.

In the entryway shelves where we had Daddy's bowling trophies, she had wild carvings made of stone and clay. Some had lips that pouched out and giant circle earrings; others had potbellies. A woman's breasts were round bulges, barely stuck on. A man's thing stuck straight out in front, like a small third arm, pointing. I hurried by it and tripped over a rug in the living room.

Her shelves were filled with Indian pots and shiny black boxes decorated with polished stones or tiny fairy-tale paintings. A globe sat on a stand in one corner. I looked for Guatemala. It was orange. In another corner, a carved tusk curved toward me, taller than I was. I felt sorry for the elephant, having that heavy thing growing out of its face. There wasn't any television. It was an enchanted house. I wanted to memorize it, to take it home, and in the darkness before I fell asleep, to walk around in it again and touch everything and open the books and boxes.

Thick picture books of paintings, not *Reader's Digests* like at our house, were spread out on the coffee table. On the cover of one called *Pre-Columbian Art* was a carving just like the woman in the entryway with the round belly. Inside there might be pictures like that man figure, so I didn't open it. I watered the inside plants and then turned on the sprinkler and waited out on the patio in a hammock. Hanging over it, a yellow honeysuckle vine reminded me of Mom's crocheted shawl.

"What's pre-Columbian, Mom?" I asked while drying the dinner plates that she stood up in the sink rack.

"Before Columbian, I suppose."

"But what's that?"

"Well, you can look it up, honey."

She meant in *The Encyclopedia Americana*, a big-deal purchase that year, but it didn't have any colored pictures like *The Junior World Book* at school did. After it arrived in its too-tight bookcase, any question of mine got the same answer: Look it up. But I could barely pull the books out. I don't remember my parents ever using them.

Volume twenty-one, the Ps, said that pre-Columbian meant "Indians of Mexico and Central America in the pre-Hispanic period," whatever that was. The encyclopedia always made you look up something else to understand the first thing. Maybe in Guatemala Miss Haskin would dig up a little clay Indian, with his thing sticking straight up out of the dirt. If pre-Hispanic was old, I figured Gramp would know about it. He could even talk to Miss Haskin about it when she came home and they would like each other, and while they talked I could look around her house more. I went in to ask him, but he was asleep, breathing loudly through his open mouth.

"Jenny," he said the next day, his voice scraping like a Popsicle stick across the sidewalk. "Let me teach you to paint." I wasn't sure I wanted him to. The room smelled bad, but not just because of his cigarettes and paints. Once Mom said Gramp's blood ran with turpentine, which I thought was what made his skin waxy and yellow.

Practicing a secret style of shallow breathing, I sat on the edge of the bed and he held my hand inside his spidery one while I held the long brush. Like a miracle, in front of me appeared an unrolled white flower with an orange finger inside. "There's nothing so cheerful as a calla lily," he said as we worked. "They grow tall and straight and one day, they open themselves to the world."

"Miss Haskin has lots of pictures on her walls," I said. "No flowers, though."

"Pictures of what?"

"Stone villages and pointy churches. Kind of like castles. Maybe you can see them someday."

"Maybe."

"And talk to her about them."

I finally had to let go of my breath before he said "maybe" a second time.

Each day I explored more of Miss Haskin's house. In the den, which in the flip-flop was actually my room, books in tall bookcases were alphabetical, by author. A pink book had gold letters down the edge that said *Canterbury Tales*. I thought it might be children's stories or fairy tales. I lifted it out carefully so it wouldn't leave a pathway in the dust. It wasn't even English but almost was. I knew it would be useless to ask Mom what it meant. She'd only say, "Look it up, honey." Sitting right out there next to an atlas stood *The Communist Manifesto*. I didn't know what manifesto meant, but I knew the first word well enough. I sure wasn't going to tell that to anyone. Miss Haskin could count on me.

After a few days the mail piled up below the slot in the door so I carried it over to the dining room table and stacked it according to size. Then I thought she might want to know what order it came in, so I rearranged it. Her first name, I learned, was Harriet. I felt included in a secret. Even Mom called her Miss Haskin. One letter called her Dr. H. Haskin. Two letters had foreign stamps. Scotland and Mexico. I could hardly believe she knew people there.

I moved the sprinkler from the ivy to the grass and settled in the hammock with a giant book. *Picasso*. The name reminded me of piccolo. It had paintings of people, but all stretched out, with the faces rearranged. On page 107 was a picture of a crazy woman. She wore a crumpled red hat with a blue flower, and her hair hung in long purple and green ropes behind petal ears. Her skin glowed the bright yellow-green of honeysuckles where the blossom joins the stem, but her nose sat crooked and her big mouth was a bunch of angles. Her fingers clutched at her teeth. She looked about to explode. Under it was printed, "'Woman Weeping,' oil, 1937."

Her mouth reminded me of Miss Haskin. I wanted to bring it home to show Gramp but thought it might make him not like her. His paintings weren't like that at all. He only painted farms and mountains that didn't make the world so jangled.

"You were gone a long time," Mom said when I came home.

She gave me the narrow-eyed, Eleventh Commandment look. I had already been taught the Old Testament Extensions. Honor thy father and thy mother included thy great-grandfather, and after my cousin's family got a new car, the Tenth was, "Thou shalt not covet thy neighbor's house nor his ox nor his ass nor anything else in thy neighbor's garage." I knew it also meant anything in Miss Haskin's living room. Mom's look told me the Eleventh: "Thou shalt not be nosy."

"I was watching television," I muttered.

"Go in and talk to Gramp, will you, Jenny? He needs some company."

Gramp wobbled his head when I came in and squished out another cigarette. "Hi," I said, trying to make one breath last as long as I could.

His hand, like a spiky leaf all dried up, reached out under my Dutch girl quilt and clamped onto my arm. "You did your lessons good today, Jenny?"

"Gramp, it's summer. School's out."

"Oh." His fingers loosened, but he didn't let go. "Where were you then?"

"Miss Haskin's." He looked flat under the sheet. I didn't understand how he could have a pointy thing or where it went. I looked away. On his easel was a small painting of a mountain lake with tall needle trees, a flock of sheep, and clouds. "It looks peaceful," I said. "Where's that, Gramp?"

"Gilead."

I'd never heard of it, but thought it might be in Montana where he went on a painting trip once.

"It's nice." He looked at me, almost into me, as if his greatest wish was that I had meant what I said. "I like it. Have you ever heard of Picasso?" I asked. He nodded. "What do you know about him?"

"Paints like a crazy man." The way he sliced out the words surprised me so I didn't say anything more. It made me worry that when Miss Haskin came home, they wouldn't like each other, and then I wouldn't be able to go over there anymore.

Sometime in the middle of the night Gramp started to snore differently, with wheezing breaths, sometimes sudden and gagging. I put the pillow over my head to make a soft, cool cave. In the darkness I saw Gramp's face rearranged, his ears upside down, his eyes at weird angles. His face was yellow.

What I heard that night made me go to Miss Haskin's earlier the next day. Her mail was a postcard invitation to something at a gallery and a letter from Maine. I looked it up in her atlas and found it wasn't close to Montana at all. The states didn't believe in alphabetical order. I started the sprinkler and took a fat book called *Romantic Painting* to the patio and sank down in the hammock, thinking I'd enjoy pictures of couples in old-fashioned clothes holding hands in parks or on sailboats. I opened the book and my skin crawled cold. A man with a rag wrapped around his tipped head was lying in a box or a bathtub with a board across it like a table. He held a letter in one hand and a feather pen in the other, but he was dead, or dying. A tiny, maroon cut in his chest leaked a trickle of blood. The bath water looked like raspberry juice. The way light fell on him, his skin, the sheet behind him, and his head rag all glowed with the same color, a pale greenish yellow. My stomach cramped. Gramp's skin. "The Death of Marat," it was called. It gave me the chills, it was so real. I knew it wouldn't be good for me to look at it but I couldn't stop myself.

In the corner of my eye I saw a trickle of water, like the blood stream, running across the cement under the hammock. I'd forgotten the sprinkler and flooded the ivy.

"How did you learn of Picasso?" Gramp asked one morning when I went in to get clean clothes.

"From one of Miss Haskin's books. She has books with paintings in them that I look at sometimes."

He watched me with a weak smile. "Good. You do that, Jenny."

"Why are you mad at him?"

"At who?"

"Mr. Picasso."

"I'm not. He just caused a lot of changes, and it was hard for me, that's all." I gathered underwear, socks, my plaid shorts, and a red shirt. "What else does Miss Haskin have?" he asked.

"Lots of things. Carvings and pots. I wish you could see them." I glanced toward the door, not wanting Mom to hear how nosy I was. "Do you think someday you'd feel good enough to go with me?"

"No, Jenny. That wouldn't be right."

"Then after she gets back?"

"Yes, maybe then, if—." He stopped, right like that.

"If what?"

"Nothing."

It was Miss Haskin's den I wanted to explore most. That afternoon I just stood there and stared, in case she came back early. A plaque awarded to Harriet Haskin, PhD, hung on the wall. "For Excellence in Teaching, College of Arts and Letters, June 1951," it said. A school just for writing letters. No wonder she had so much mail. On a small table there was a typewriter, something we didn't have.

I tiptoed to her desk. In a gold frame there was a photo of a young couple sitting in a skinny boat. In the back of it was a man wearing a striped shirt holding a pole. It was in a stone city all carved into curves and frills. I bent over it closely. The man wore a squared-off straw hat and the woman a flowered dress. I'd never seen Miss Haskin in a flowered dress, but that stretched-out smile had to be hers. Her teeth were whoppers and her jaw jutted out at an angle. She looked happy, but she wasn't pretty, just young. It made me sad for her.

I wondered if there were more pictures. I opened the desk drawer about four inches, slowly, so it wouldn't make any noise. I didn't breathe. It creaked and I froze. The Eighth, Thou shalt not steal, pounded in my head. I shoved the drawer closed. It wasn't that I wanted to take anything. I just wanted to know.

Practically the only sound in our house all day was Gramp's wheezing and sometimes a weak little cough that scraped at my ears. Miss Haskin wasn't due back for a week and every day Gramp seemed further and further away. I hated it.

"What's archeology really?" I asked him after I'd waited an hour for him to wake up.

"Just what you're doing next door, Jenny. Digging up things. Then putting them together."

"Why do they do it?"

"To make a picture of a world." The words came out in scratchy spurts, as if it hurt, and I had to lean close to hear through the whistle in his chest. "Archeologists are scientists who do it for whole civilizations, and you're doing it for one person." He choked but it seemed like he wanted to keep talking. "Or maybe you're doing it for a civilization, too, come to think of it."

If I memorized what he said, maybe someday I'd understand it. I waited for some sign, for permission to ask one more question. I touched the back of his hand and the skin felt unconnected to the bones. His soft eyes lifted and looked directly at me. "Do you think it's wrong that I'm nosy?"

"No, Jenny. Look at everything. Always," he whispered.

So I said hi to the pre-Columbian figures when I let myself in the next day, took a closer look at the man, and reached for some letters on the floor. One square blue envelope was pretty lumpy so I squeezed it a little, then gasped. It was addressed to Peaches Haskin. This was something I knew I shouldn't see. Who would dare call her that? D. Cheney, the return address said. From Canada. Nobody like Gramp, I was sure. Maybe D. Cheney read *The Communist Manifesto* too. I crept back home as if I'd stolen something, but my empty hands were only sweaty.

Gramp held a brush and stared out the window to the backyard. It didn't look like he had done anything on Gilead. Since he didn't notice me, I looked long, to remember him for all time. The whiskery skin of his throat hung in loose folds like a turkey. I wished he looked nicer.

I went outside to Miss Haskin's back fence and came back in. "Here's some raspberries," I said, and laid a bowlful on his bed. "They're Miss Haskin's. I just picked them." As if from a faraway country, he turned to me slowly and hardly smiled, and in that moment I was afraid. I watched his long fingernails grasp for the berries, watched as he laid them on his tongue, watched as his eyes swam. He ate like a robot, concentrating on each one, and left one in the bowl.

"For you, Jenny." I shook my head. He pushed the bowl toward me and his mouth did a little jerk. As I ate it, my tongue found the soft hole at the top, and the sections of Gramp's last berry sprang apart in my mouth.

I didn't know how long Gramp would last and I got confused about what to wish for—Miss Haskin to come back soon so Gramp could know her, or her to stay away longer so I could keep going to her house. The next day I took a piece of notebook paper folded in my pocket. I set the sprinkler going and went into my room, the den. The typewriter was still there. The chair creaked when I sat down but I didn't even jump. My paper rolled in crooked. It took a long time to find the letters. They weren't in alphabetical order. "Jenny Cochran," I typed. The keys went down a long way before they printed, and I pressed them unevenly. Every so often the typewriter skipped a space. I started again. "Miss Jennifer Cochran." Then, "Miss Harriet Haskin." Underneath that, "Peaches Haskin." "Dr. Peaches Haskin." Then, "Miss Jennifer Haskin."

I rolled out the paper and on the way home I tore it into tiny pieces.

The next morning when I woke up, Gramp's door was closed. Mom usually opened it a crack first thing in the morning to hear him if he needed anything. I suddenly felt hot and cold at the same time. It couldn't be yet. It was too soon. I found Mom in the kitchen, just standing there holding onto the sink. She nodded, then told me to go to Miss Haskin's and stay until she called me on the phone.

In Miss Haskin's entryway, the pre-Columbian figures went all squiggly. He didn't wait. Through the blur of the hallway, I saw his turkey neck and Miss Haskin's flamingo legs and the woman with the purple hair and the man in the bathtub and Mom and Dad too, who probably didn't even know about the bathtub man. I used up about six tissues. I tried not to because she only had a few left. Then I didn't know what to do with them. I couldn't leave them there— she'd find out I was in her bathroom—so I stuffed them in my Keds.

I knew why I'd been sent here—so I wouldn't see, but that was just what I wanted. I had to find out if Gramp's arm was hanging over the side of the bed, like the man in the tub. I snuck into the house through the back door. Mom was on the phone, talking in a low, serious voice. Who did she think would hear? I held my breath and turned the knob at Gramp's room and cracked open the door just enough to see his face. The yellow had faded from his face, and his skin looked like crumpled wax paper. His arm was under the covers. I ran back to Miss Haskin's and dove onto her bed.

He'd seen a lot of things—Gilead and Montana, places I knew nothing about —and I hadn't even asked him. And he didn't get to know Miss Haskin. So when she came home, that would be it.

I lay there sideways for a long time, until the wet spot on her bedspread was cold and clammy next to my cheek. I rolled onto my back and looked around at the most inside place of her house. Of course, it was filled with treasures. Lying there where she slept, with all the world around me, I knew I didn't need to cry for her.

When Mom called me home, hours later but too soon, he was gone. Our house didn't breathe. The bedroom door and window were wide open but the curtains weren't blowing so I still smelled turpentine and death in that room, my room I guess it was now. Mom had the bed stripped and was putting on clean sheets, my favorites, the ones with the daisies. But he had slept in them the week before. His easel was gone, and unfinished Gilead was propped against the closet door. His jar of brushes stood on the bedside table. When Mom left, I took the longest one, wrapped it in tissue and hid it in my bottom drawer.

That night I sat a long time on the living room rug. Mom knew why and made up the sofa again.

Several mornings later while I folded the blanket in the living room, I watched out our bay window as Miss Haskin flapped down the pathway to our front door. Too late. I hugged the blanket to my chest and didn't breathe. Maybe she'd forget to ask for her key. She had oxfords on, just like mine, but she was a lady of the world. When Mom called me outside to the porch, I felt suddenly shy, afraid Miss Haskin could read on my face what I knew about her.

"Did you have a good time—digging?" I asked, looking at a scab on her hand.

"It was wonderful. I mean full of wonder."

I knew what she meant, and was able to look at her face smiling down at me. "Did you bring anything back?"

My disappointment in learning that any treasure would be kept in a museum was interrupted by Mom announcing that Gramp had died. My throat tightened into a double knot. Miss Haskin's voice was deep when she said she was sorry. It wasn't her fault. Nobody said anything for a minute, and I noticed she tied her oxfords with four loops just like I did. "Death can be a rich experience," she said.

Mom's back straightened into her I-don't-quite-like-what-you-said posture. I would need time to figure it out. For anyone else to say that, it would be weird, but not for Miss Haskin.

She thanked me for watering and said I did a good job, that the plants looked healthier and had grown a lot. She held out three dollar bills. My hand would not go up to take the money. "Take this, Jennifer. Please." Her low voice floated down and surrounded me like the honeysuckle in her patio. If I didn't take it, she might think I didn't like her. I forced my hand toward her. For a second, both our hands were on the stiff dollar bills.

"Gramp wanted to see your picture books." The words spilled out before I thought them. "On pre-Columbian art." I turned my face so I wouldn't see Mom. Miss Haskin didn't look at her either.

"I'm sorry," she said again. "But you can. Anytime."

I closed my eyes and let out a breath.

That night I stood on the back deck and knew I would not spend the three dollars for a long, long time. I think Gramp would agree that they would make good bookmarks. Beyond the raspberry fence, light from the den window next door shone out on the ivy. Peaches Haskin was probably reading her mail. I went into my bedroom, turned on the light, and opened the curtains so the light from my window spread over our backyard, too. I took one of Gramp's sketch pads, climbed into bed, and drew a jumbled face with an enormous, crooked mouth and purple hair. I didn't make the eyes match. Below it I printed, "'Miss Haskin Reading,' crayon, 1955."

Photo by Jeanette Easton

my grandfather played a piano made of teeth
Katharyn Howd Machan

and wood dark as promise
from glass-lipped Bohemia
that a man who makes music
matters

to a world and a woman
whose love dared to cross
polished keyboard
with touch that tried

class? send her away
get her to America
who could imagine
he would follow

Ohio midnights
eight hands playing
songs and symphonies
Father decreed

his daughters taught
and never married
his sons shaped lives
of hard black notes

my brother spins records
I dance to poems
their story
still scoring our years

photograph of my grandfather
Carolyn Marie Souaid

Somehow, in the middle of the Turkish War
he found time to pose for the camera
eyes staring squarely into the lens
bullets bandoliered across his lean chest.

He is a young man, *kefaya* draped
in elegant folds around his head, rifle locked
in his arm, feet slightly apart, waiting for the click
of the shutter.

Though he doesn't know it, he carries generations
in the sepia grain of his flesh—my mother, my aunts and
  uncles
my cousins, the lot of us his chromosome army
charging into infinity.

I knew him as a quiet man who boiled eggs for lunch
and wore long johns to bed. The *jiddo* who taught me checkers
in his noisy den off Spadina. I loved the smell of that room
the blue tins of Edgeworth tobacco. I loved the way
his long, hairless finger tapped the rosewood pipe

the way his sharp blue eye
never once left the game.

Photo by Jeffrey Swanberg

the truck
Randeane Tetu

"Get your revs up," Grandpa said. "Get your revs up."

The truck hovered and huffed and swallowed and stalled. I stepped on the brake and the truck stopped and all of the hayfield stayed still around us where a certain softness of evening came from the trees at the bottom of the field and a certain brightness stood in the hay stubble and leaned underneath the trees that started the woods at the top of the field.

"Okay," he said. "You've got to keep your revs up. Push in the clutch and give it some gas."

"Now?"

"Not now. When it acts like that. Now you're going to have to start it."

"Okay." I pushed in the clutch and stepped on the gas and turned the key off and then on, and the truck rolled a little backward and started and I caught it on the brake.

"Well, girl, you're learning how to start it," Grandpa said.

The hay stubble wasn't damp with evening yet, but it was damp enough to skid the tires starting uphill and so, listening to the engine, I edged off the clutch and held the brake, then let it go for the gas and gave it too much, and we rolled backward, and I let off the clutch, and the tires skittered enough that the truck didn't stall but slid a little sideward, and started forward.

Grandpa let go of the armrest and put both hands in his lap. "Okay," he said. "That was better."

I stayed in first gear until he said, "Shift," and I shifted into second.

The three-acre field seemed mostly uphill, but of course there was just as much downhill. I just didn't notice the downhill much because the truck didn't want to stall on the downhill.

Grandpa was looking forward through the windshield while I drove around the outside edge of the field. I didn't try third and the truck didn't stall.

"Did you teach my mother how to drive when she was ten?" I asked.

"Yes, sure I taught her," he said, coming back from wherever he'd been out the window. "And she learned a lot faster than you."

"She said it took her forever."

"I don't remember that."

"That's just what she said."

"Mmm," he said and went to looking back out the window. I came to the birches and turned onto a level with the sun to drop the truck downhill again.

He wasn't watching for deer because they wouldn't come out with the noise we were making, and it was too early yet. And he wasn't seeing the stone in the field with the spout of grass above it or he'd say he should someday take it out.

He maybe was looking at the corner of the field that dipped down to the lane toward the barns and, after that, the house. But we came to that corner and he didn't look at that either. He kept on out the window and I thought his shadow flew across the stubble, but it was only one of those crows.

"I saw her, Grandpa," I said. "It's all right. I saw her."

"You saw who?" He sounded cranky.

I don't usually tell my dreams. But Grandpa was looking out the window that way he had of not looking at anything that was there. And I had started wanting the Klondike Bar he had in his freezer for me. Unless he told me to shift into third, I wasn't going to stall the truck anymore tonight and so we might as well drive back down the lane where at least I could look out for trees.

"Who'd you see?" he asked.

"I saw Grandma Addie," I said. "She's all right." I knew he missed her something awful since she'd died.

Grandpa turned to look at me and the truck did a couple of sidesteps on the corner to start uphill, but I didn't panic and gave it less gas and it climbed steady up to the top. Grandpa looked out through the windshield again.

"What do you mean, you saw her?" he asked.

"In my dream, I saw her." We crossed the top of the hayfield and rounded the corner and started back downhill. The bottom was in shadow from the line of trees and the evening light seemed to tilt across them in dots and lines.

Coming up, things looked gold with a little red coming out of the trees and shadow. And the woods at the top looked lit underneath and standing up on the light.

"You saw her in what dream?" Grandpa asked. He was looking at me, and I had the truck going smooth underneath us across the top of the hayfield.

"Well, two dreams, actually, that I know of." The truck was going so smooth I took one hand off the wheel. But then I put it right back on and we came to the corner and started down. The truck made a funny checkered holding-back noise but I didn't give it any more gas. "The first dream was the night she died. I could see her walking under the trees. Not these trees. Some trees that started high up. I mean their branches started high up. On both sides of a lane. And there was a wind." We were in darkness, now, that the trees laid across the lower part of the field. I was starting to see the track we were making where we'd broken down the grass and dust came through. "She was very young," I said. "And she was walking and there was a lot of wind that pulled her skirt. Her hair was brown instead of grey."

We came to the part where the truck dug in at the corner to climb up again. We had worn off a couple of places and I tried not to dig them out more.

Grandpa looked through the windshield. He held onto the armrest.

The red light was dying down a little in the space beneath the trees at the top and catching on the leaves of the laurel bushes a way that I hadn't noticed last time.

"Is it all right to tell you I saw her?" I asked.

"What other time did you see her?"

"A few days after that. I only saw her face that time, upside down. She was leaning out of the haymow and smiling at me as if she'd done something grand. It made me remember the word 'imp' to see her look down like that."

"Imp?" he said. "Did you say 'imp'?" Now Grandpa was looking at me.

"Imp," I said. "I'm sorry if I shouldn't have told you." I was holding onto the steering wheel now because of how he was looking at me. He still held onto the armrest, but he leaned away from it toward me and I looked back at the track we were making around the hayfield.

"I don't know what made me think it," I said. "It's just the word I thought when I saw her looking full of herself and leaning down to look at me."

We crossed the top and started down and Grandpa looked over the trees. He wasn't looking where we were going and he wasn't holding onto the armrest. It looked to me farther than ever to the Klondike Bar.

I don't tell people my dreams because then they ask me questions that I can't answer. So I've learned to be quiet about them. I guess I should have been quiet because Grandpa isn't even noticing how dark it's getting. When we lift to the top of the field, we're still in shadow and the wishing star has been set out on the air. He has both hands between his knees and his head to the side a little. I start hoping he's okay.

When I'm driving, he never lets me think that I'm in charge, and he's gruff if I ask to go into another gear or anything else he doesn't tell me. Otherwise, I could decide on my own to pull the headlights on, which I've never done before, or to drive down the lane toward the barns.

I suddenly feel as if I'm all alone driving in the truck and it startles me. I turn my head and see him still sitting there. He hasn't really changed how he looks but his looks have somehow changed. Maybe it's the darkness that softens his face with just that little light from the sky.

I can still see where I am going, and the path we've made looks lighter in the dark and the truck takes on a rhythm I can feel with my feet and hands.

Suddenly, I know I am driving. "This is what it is," I think, and something that I don't think about shifts us into third at the top of the hill. It is smooth, so smooth, with my foot on the clutch, and the shift lever in my hand, and this driving-self of me shoots ahead through the windshield. When Grandpa stirs, I can hardly fit back inside the truck.

"Just like that," my grandpa says. I turn to him and my chest is wider than the truck, and he smiles. Now I'm the one who wants to ask what he means.

Drive the truck just like that? Or her face up in the haymow would look just like my face looked, full of myself, when he turned and saw me driving? But I've learned not to say things right away that might spoil something by being answered, and that gives me the moment I need to let the thought catch up that it could be both of these things I'm thinking.

And so I nod and I don't ask him and he points at the field that is covered in downy dark. "You pull your headlights on, why don't you? And head back down toward home."

The headlights look dry on the trunks of the trees and I steer in the ruts the tractor has made going down the lane. Then the other field opens out and we're on a level with the sky and the stars come down around the barns and the house.

"You know where to find that Klondike Bar," he says and I steer the truck onto the driveway.

I push in the clutch and stop with the brake, right by the steps that go up to the porch. He reaches his foot to take the brake from me and pushes the shift into neutral. No lights are on in the house.

I drop out of the truck and close the door. Grandpa sets the seat back in notches and puts the truck into first.

I find the Klondike Bar in the freezer in the light from the refrigerator door and sit out on the porch with it. The sky is darker.

Grandpa is still driving around the field and I guess he's looking at stars. I hear every time he shifts into second at the lower corner and back up to third at the top.

grandma at markleeville
Jennifer Lagier

Beside a subtle trickle
of melting snowpack
our two fishermen
leave us tending the fire
while they patiently angle.
Despite the living bridge
of her son,
the man I call father,
she and I have never connected
and remain total strangers.
We sit back at the quiet campsite,
testing the waters by casting
bright spinners of family stories.
Invisible under the Sierra stars,
she lights that surprising
and forbidden cigarette,
conjures red Tennessee dirt
and the fairy-tale forests.
Like an agile trout,
the jaws of her images
bump and tease,
miss the mind's hook;
today, I only vaguely remember.
Grandma's voice shimmers briefly
then disappears in the forking flow
beneath rolling years
of the tumbling water.

Photo by Marianne Gontarz

the orange popsicle
Catherine Mellett

Rose Hennessey wore her wheat-colored hair in a braided bun, like the rest of the Irish women in our neighborhood. The braid was twisted in the shape of a fancy Easter bread and shot through with fine silver strands that caught the light when she talked. Occasionally, a hairpin slipped as if lifted by a graceful hand, fell to her shoulder, and bounced onto the floor, soundlessly.

She was a tiny woman, and in that certain way a good friend for a child to have. My mother rented out rooms in our house, and Rose lived in two of them. Her kitchen windows were at the back of our house and looked across the Ohio River to the city. All summer long, we pulled her kitchen chairs up to the windows and sat side by side, as if we were watching a movie. From there, we could see the old men fishing, the incline train on Mount Washington taking people home, the coal barges going back and forth on the river.

"I wish there was something I could give you," she said, one hot day in July. I wasn't sure if this was a reference to my eleventh birthday, which had just passed, or the fact that I was grounded again and she felt sorry for me.

I don't remember what I had done that time to get my mother mad, but I was really just as happy inside the house as outside. I had won the top prize in art class that year. The last day of school, when my art teacher gave me the award, she told me that I had been nominated to attend Saturday morning art classes at the museum starting in the fall. I would get a scholarship. All I had to do was get my mother to fill out the application and sign it. I had the application in my room, waiting for the time when my mother would cool down. As far as I was concerned, being grounded didn't matter. I could sit and draw anywhere.

Right when school ended, my father left us in the lurch again, departing for places unknown. Sometimes I drew him, as it had to be, from memory, but most often I drew objects around me. Whenever I was grounded I took my paper and pencils and climbed the three flights of stairs to visit Rose and drew what I could see from her kitchen window.

Rose looked all around her kitchen that day for something to give me.

"Wait." She got up from her chair and went over to the kitchen cabinets. She opened a narrow drawer and fished around, back and forth, through unraveled spools of thread, empty gum wrappers, S&H Green Stamps, and spinster silverware. I couldn't help but be excited, thinking of what she might find. The beautician, who lived on the other side of our house, had once given me a Japanese paper fan she found lying at the bottom of her closet, discarded, as if it were an unimportant thing. My mother made me give it back because she didn't want me to accept anything from the tenants. That was one of her rules.

Rose closed the drawer and looked at the ancient ivory-colored icebox leaning on its hind legs in the corner. She opened the door and poked through old pieces of aluminum foil. "Oh, that's right," she said, looking amused. "I forgot. I don't have anything today."

After I finished drawing, we sat looking at the river. "Listen!" she said. I sat very silent beside her, making sure not to move a muscle. She patted my chest. "I hear your little heart, just a-beating away." I listened and heard the thump-thumping, too.

"*I* know," she said, all excited. "I'm going to buy you something." She got up from her chair, determined. "Let's go to Metzger's and pick out something you like."

"Oh, no," I said. I knew my mother would be angry. "I don't want anything. I can't accept it." I said this as images of colored pencils and drawing paper flashed through my head.

"And *why* not?" she said. Her eyes were a misty blue-grey like swirly marbles. "Why can't you accept it?" she asked. "Why?"

I lowered my eyes.

What was the right answer? I couldn't tell her the real reason: *Because you are poor. Because you have less than we do, and we should be giving to you.* That answer, I knew, would hurt her feelings. I felt ashamed because I guessed that she already knew the answer my mother had taught me.

"I don't know," I finally said. "I just can't."

She turned and went into her bed-sitting-room, a triangular slice of a room across from the stairway at the top of our house. There was a low black horse-hair couch that she slept on, a mahogany table and a lamp, and a rocker in the corner near the narrow window. These had all belonged to us at one time or another. On the table was a photograph of her daughter, Amy, who had died with her husband and child in a car accident.

I watched as Rose got ready to go out. She took off her floral-printed house-dress and full cotton apron. Then she put on layer after layer of black cotton clothing, which she wrapped around herself in a complicated fashion. I helped with the white cotton wraps that went around her knees. I always helped with those. Finally, she put on her black shoes, which looked like big slabs of heavy cardboard.

"Come on, then," she said when she was ready. "I need some company."

All the way down the stairs, I thought about whether it would be better to go with her or to stay. I remembered how red my mother's face became when she saw the Japanese fan. I told her that the beautician didn't want it anymore because it had been a present from an old boyfriend, a merchant marine. This story, which seemed so exciting to me, only made my mother angrier.

When we got outside and were ready to cross the street, I chickened out. "I can't go! She'll kill me," I said, being as dramatic as my mother usually was.

"I doubt she'll do that," Rose said. "All right. Make an old lady walk down the hill alone."

As I lay on the front lawn waiting for her, I watched the clouds passing over-head. After I fell into a half-sleep, she put a small bag into my hand. Through the brown paper, I felt the hard, beveled coldness. I looked inside. There were two. Two orange Popsicles. She didn't have any other groceries.

"You take one," I said.

"I can't eat those. I got them for you. Enjoy them."

As I started to take one of the Popsicles out of the bag, I turned toward the house.

The curtain in an upstairs window moved and my mother, half-cast in shadow, was turning away. Her mouth looked like an upside-down smile. It was the look that always made my heart feel as if it had been squeezed. She flung the curtain back against the window. I expected her to be outside in a moment, so I tried to get rid of the evidence.

"Here!" I said, pushing the bag back into Rose's hands. "I can't take this," I said again, trying to sound polite.

"Now what do you suppose I should do with these? I bought them for you." She stood in front of me. Her old black skirt was at my eye level. I could see her white knee wraps peeking out from beneath. Her shoes looked gnarled like old stumps, and the area around the toes had little hills where the leather had molded to the shape of her huge corns. "Don't you want them?"

I shook my head, no.

That night at dinner, my mother talked to me as if she were continuing a conversation we had been having. "Popsicles are seven cents apiece, which isn't much to us, but it's a lot to Rose Hennessey. The next time that poor old lady offers you something, take it, for God's sake. Don't insult her."

I could only look at her.

She looked back at me triumphantly. She had just curled her auburn hair and it stood out in waves from her face.

"I saw you out there," she said. "I can't believe you'd let her go by herself all that way to the store. You know she's old. And then to refuse what she has to give you—as if it isn't good enough. Yes, that's the way you act, as if things aren't good enough for you. Well, they're in the freezer, so you'd better eat them."

I had brought the application with me to the table, but this, I knew, was not a good time to ask her for anything. When she got up to get more coffee, I slid the application under the place mat.

"What's that?" she asked, taking a sip of coffee.

"Nothing," I said.

"That's that piece of paper you've been carrying around. What are you keeping from me now?"

I told her about the classes.

"Let me see it," she said. She put her hand up to her temple as she read.

"What does it cost?"

"Nothing," I told her. "It's free."

She looked skeptical. "There must be some catch."

"No, there isn't. All I have to pay for are my supplies."

"Great! As if we have money for that!" She folded the paper and left it on the table as she got up to clear away the dishes.

"So, are you going to sign it?" I asked, trying to be as casual as possible.

"I have to think about it," she said.

"It won't cost anything."

"That's what you always say. Everything costs nothing to you. But when all these little things are added up, they cost a lot. I told you I'd think about it. Besides, you'll need bus fare. That costs something. And I don't know if I like you going to East Liberty alone on the bus."

I pointed out that I traveled farther than that to school every day—just in the other direction.

"I told you I'd think about it,'" she said. "I don't like that neighborhood for a young girl."

The next night, I went downstairs as soon as I heard my mother come home from work. I went into the living room with the application, planning to keep trying until I wore her down.

She was sitting at her desk with her back to me.

"Mom, I really want to go to that school," I began. "I spend all day drawing."

When she turned around I saw that her face was red and that she was crying. She had a letter in her hand.

"They found your father," she said. A strange smile crossed her face. "They found him with his rotten woman. They're in San Francisco now. He says he's not going to give us any more money. Just like that. He's not going to."

She got a tissue from the top drawer of her desk and blew her nose. Then she started crying all over again.

She looked at the letter. "He said, 'Just try to put me in jail for desertion. It's not as bad as being in jail with you.' That's what I sit up at night worrying about. The fact that he can have a child and just leave it with nothing."

"He'll be back," I told her. "You said so yourself. He always comes back, Mom."

She got up and smiled at me, a bitter smile, and went upstairs.

I took the application into the kitchen and left it there on the table.

The next day, when I woke up, I went to see if she had signed it. I stood leaning over the kitchen table in my pajamas when she came into the room.

"That's just going to cost more money," she said. Her face was swollen and her voice sounded tired. She was taking her pink rollers out of her hair.

"No, it's not," I said. "It's really not. I have most of the supplies. You can give me less lunch money one day, and that will make up for the bus fare."

She went back to her bedroom to finish fixing her hair.

Absentmindedly, I sat down and began drinking a glass of orange juice that was on the kitchen table.

When she came back in, dressed and ready for work, she said, "You didn't drink the orange juice, did you? That's the last glass." She picked up the glass and looked at it. "You don't even like orange juice. That's great, I can't even have a glass of orange juice to myself." She sat down and began to cry.

When I went upstairs to see Rose I didn't take my pens and papers, but I did tell her the whole story, leaving nothing out, not even the orange juice.

"Your mother is so young," she said. "She has too much responsibility. This big house . . . and she doesn't have anyone to help her."

She thought for a moment and then said, "Let's see this application."

I went to my room and brought it back. When she saw that it was just a mimeographed form made up by the school, she said, "Eh! This is nothing. It's your father she's upset about."

"Oh, him," I said, confidently. *"He'll* be back. He always comes back. There's usually not a woman involved, though."

She looked at me with such a solid stare it made me uncomfortable.

"But if I don't get this form back in time," I said, "they won't let me in."

"To be so young again and to have such worries." She shook her head and laughed and asked me to get her a pen.

We sat at her kitchen table filling out the application. She read the form over and said to me, "Look, here," pointing at the bottom. "It says signature. It doesn't say *whose* now, does it?" She took the pen from me and winked. I watched as she signed my mother's name.

"Come fall, your mother will regret that she let you pass up this opportunity."

"She'll know . . . " I began.

"You let me worry about that," Rose said. "Now we'll mail this, and I'll talk to her about it later when she's feeling better."

We rooted around in her kitchen drawers for a long time until we found a stamp. When we walked to the mailbox, it was dusk and we felt like two conspirators sneaking out in the night. On the way home, I started feeling anxious, but when we stopped on the steps she said, "Now don't let on what we cooked up here, okay?" With this, I felt that somehow everything would fall into place, that I would start attending classes in the fall and my mother would forget she ever had to sign anything. I'd leave it all to Rose, another adult, to smooth things over with my mother.

About two weeks later, I came home after my mother got back from work. The mail was strewn about the hall table, and my mother's shoes were lying at odd angles in the middle of the hallway. A crumpled envelope was on the top of the pile of bills and magazines. I saw the museum's return address.

I listened for my mother's voice and thought I heard the two of them talking upstairs. I crept up the stairs and sat on the stairway, holding on to the banister.

"It seems that everyone wants to interfere in my life," my mother was saying. "Do I interfere in yours? Do I come into your room and go through your things?"

"Of course not."

"That's what this is like."

"Well, don't blame Katie, blame me," Rose said. "I know now I shouldn't have done it, but at the time I didn't think you'd mind."

My mother said something I couldn't hear.

"It's just that I worry about Katie," Rose said.

"*You* worry about her?" my mother said.

"Yes, I do," said Rose, firmly.

My mother started to leave.

"Like those Popsicles," Rose said. "I could see she wanted them but she wouldn't take them. They were just a little present from an old lady, and you would have thought the child was making the choice of a lifetime. She couldn't even accept—"

"You're wrong," my mother said. "Katie didn't want them. She just didn't want to hurt your feelings. I had to put them in the trash, they made such a mess."

"Well," Rose said. "I'm sorry to have created such a problem for you.

"I *tell* Katie not to accept things from our tenants."

"Oh, Peggy," Rose said. "I don't feel like a tenant. Sometimes I feel like she's my own little granddaughter."

"Well, she's not," my mother said. "You pay rent here, and you have to remember that she's not."

I sat there and listened hard, thinking there was more to come.

Finally I heard my mother say, in the same tone of voice she had used so often with my father, "I have the feeling it will never be the same between us, Rose. You've just gone too far."

"Oh, come on, Peggy," Rose said, chiding her. "It isn't as serious as you're making it out to be."

"Oh, yes, it is."

"But why?"

"You don't know why?" my mother said. "Well, then, I guess that's the problem. I'm sorry, Rose," she said softly, "I don't think things can ever be the same between us."

My mother found me sitting on the stairs and pulled me down to our part of the house. She didn't say anything until we got to the living room.

"I told you not to bother her. You have to learn to listen to me. I don't want you to go up there ever again. See the trouble you've caused?"

I stayed away from Rose for almost a whole month. But I eventually began visiting my friend again, first in secret then openly, and always careful to neither give nor take anything my mother would consider too costly or that I failed to completely understand. By the time I was back in school, I was visiting Rose again on a regular basis, while my mother, caught up in the details of trying to find my father after he left San Francisco, scarcely looked at my actions.

One Saturday morning, I found Rose in her room, lying so still on the couch that I imagined my mother had put her to sleep there like a little doll and that Rose was just waiting for my mother to come and get her up again to take her to play.

When I went in she looked up at me and said something I didn't understand at first. I came closer to her.

"Amy," she was saying. She looked so happy then. "Amy, it *is* you. You've come."

She had had a stroke. She was taken to the hospital in an ambulance. We visited her there only once. After she came back she was better for a little while but then got worse, sometimes wandering out of the house in the middle of the night. Since Rose had little money and no relatives, it was determined that she should be placed in a state nursing home for the aged. My mother, who was named the responsible party, said she was not in a position to help Rose anymore and filled out all of the appropriate papers.

Years later, I ran into the beautician who had lived in our house. I was going to lunch with some other secretaries when I saw her. I told them to go on without me. The beautician and I stopped to talk on a busy street corner. We talked about the old house and the neighborhood and about my mother, who never remarried. I brought up Rose Hennessey.

"God, how your mother loved that woman," the beautician said, shaking her head. "She was so good to her. *You* remember. Chicken dinner every Sunday. Taking her to that home . . . that was the hardest thing your mother ever did."

After I left the beautician, I remembered the day Rose Hennessey offered me those Popsicles. And, in my mind, I take one. I don't hesitate at all. We sit down and talk on the front steps. It is very hot and I eat the orange Popsicle right there in the front yard with her, enjoying it. She laughs when I take a bite and wince at the shock of the cold. After I'm finished, we go upstairs to her rooms to watch the river.

Photo by Lori Burkhalter-Lackey

suddenly the dumpster
Davi Walders

Suddenly the dumpster, there, across the street,
where for twenty years we had our older neighbor.
It hulks like a derelict in winter light.
"Associated Waste" and a grey chipped number peer
from its soot-splattered face. Hour by hour,

the rusted edges grow sharper. Box springs recoil,
a mattress shudders. Casters dangle off a dusty
damask sofa. The bladeless old mower towers
above cabinets and cans tossed later. Snow
sputters and spins, begins falling faster.

Workers shrug their shoulders. Who cares
about covers? From an upstairs window, a shoe
misses, sinking deeper. It will lie buried
with the million Tiparillos he flicked from
his rocker, there on the porch where he watched

over us. From our very first moments, he cautioned
the movers. "No," the throaty old voice, "turn,
upend that bed. Catch the cord. Don't scratch
their lamp." Then, applauding our daughter when
we brought her home. A pair, inseparable, he teaching,

she tagging through seasons that followed, until
the squirrels. It was late summer when I found them.
He'd painted their fingers and hands up to the wrist,
his bumpy and gnarled, hers smooth, still small.
They sat on the stoop, doubled in laughter, gloved

in brown peanut butter, surrounded by a thousand
furry critters nuzzling like piglets. "Rodents!"
I screamed, "rabies for God's sake." She cried
again and again wanting her friend until I gave in.
What was won was won. Now it's over. She's grown.

He's gone. His kids must have settled between
their lawyers, accepted someone's offer. Soon
all will be white detritus tucked under frozen
water. The dumpster waits for hauling. Winter
mewls its eulogy, mongering for new neighbors.

the hundred-dollar tip
Ed Weyhing

I figured the old guy was loaded. He lived in one of these houses doesn't look like much till you check out all the wings and additions and sunporches—out each side, the back, and so on—and you realize you're looking at a million, million and a half, easy. House I grew up in would have fit in the living room of this guy's house.

He was B. R. Winston, some kind of big shot businessman. Real estate? Wall Street? Junk bonds? Who knows? He was always on the society pages since he retired to Newport a few years back. My job was driving him around once a week.

Mostly I drive a cab. But best of all I like the weeklies. You get to know the people. I drive little old ladies on their errands, haul rich kids to Providence for their ballet. Conversations carry over from week to week. The little old lady tells you her life—her kids, pictures of her grandchildren. And I do great with kids. Never had a sister, just a little brother. But I'm good with the girls, too, teasing them, of course, keeping them in stitches. Relationships. It's the best part of my job.

This latest weekly was different. I figured the old guy knew something, maybe had some stories. Maybe some ideas about how I should start my limo business.

As soon as I was introduced to him I gave that up. First off he couldn't even shake hands; he barely put up his left hand. It was a stroke, and besides being paralyzed on his right side he basically couldn't talk—not so I could understand, anyway. For me it was a letdown. How can you get friendly with somebody who can't talk?

But I didn't let that set me back. "All right if I call you Lefty?" I asked. I couldn't tell if he got the joke. Instead, I got this blank look. No sense of humor, nothing.

Also, there was Millicent, the lady who took care of him. Her I couldn't figure out. She looked in good shape for a middle-aged woman. Good figure. A sharp dresser: designer slacks, expensive silk blouses, suits you wouldn't believe. Always looked as if she'd stepped in off Fifth Avenue. Except for her age, you'd never guess she dyed her hair. My mother stopped dyeing her hair after my little brother died. But back when she dyed it—you could tell, believe me.

This Millicent was too young to be his sister. Maybe his daughter, or his niece? His secretary? A nurse? For that matter, she could have been a young wife, relatively speaking. He may have even told me, but I was lucky to catch every tenth word he said. I had nothing against her personally, it was just her attitude. She always referred to him as "Mister Winston," as if I wasn't showing enough respect. But I said to myself, Louie, don't let it bother you. What does it matter, two hours a week? Hey, I'm a professional. My attitude was: do your job, get your money. I still called him Lefty.

She seemed to take good care of him. He was in his eighties, didn't seem very strong, but she always had him shined up top to toe, dressed in these expensive running shoes, some sort of matching exercise suit. Usually she was ready to go out somewhere while I drove him around.

Even though the old guy couldn't talk, the job was okay. Face it: I like to drive. After all, it's my life. Even days off, I'm in my pickup, driving somewhere. I've driven all over—Maine, New Hampshire. During slow times, I take a few days off, drive down to Atlantic City, take in a few shows, drop a little change at the tables.

In this case I drove the old guy's car, a '97 Buick, loaded with extras. Leather upholstery. It felt like sitting in a lawyer's office. A computerized voice told you everything: *The trunk is unlocked.* Or: *Fasten your seat belt.* And power? You should have felt it take the upgrade on the Newport Bridge. When you hit the top, you expected it to keep climbing, right over Jamestown.

Anyway, she laid it out for me the first day. "He enjoys riding around," she said, "seeing things."

"That's what I'm here for," I told her. Fine, lady, I thought. He enjoys riding, we'll ride. He enjoys seeing things, we'll see things.

I got him in and out of the car, no problem. I already knew how to stand a guy up out of a wheelchair, steady him into the front seat. Believe me, I've got some experience doing this. You wouldn't believe how many invalids I've hauled. After I folded his wheelchair and stashed it in the back, she handed me a brown tweed golf hat. "In case you get out of the car anywhere," she said.

I took the hat, but thought to myself, Good luck, sister! She thinks I'm going to get the old guy out? She's dreaming! You can believe I didn't want any of that responsibility. Maybe I drop him? Then he sues me, gets my license away from me? That's all I need!

That first day I took him over to the mall. There's this drive-up Foto Stop. Girl named Wanda works there. I swing through there in my cab sometimes, sit and talk till I get a call. If somebody comes up behind me, I just circle around the mall till they're finished.

I thought: He likes to drive, we can drive to the mall. He likes to see things, he can see the pair this Wanda has on her. I wondered if that had any effect on him, if he even noticed, you know, girls and all. Anyway, it was pretty obvious the old guy couldn't talk, wouldn't be telling anybody where we went, what we did or didn't do.

The next week was sunny, the Wednesday before Labor Day, and I knew there'd be fine stuff down at Easton's Beach. I drove the old guy down there, pulled right into the parking lot, into the handicapped space. Swear to God, every college girl in New England was down there. Believe me, it was a good show, and I just sat there, took it all in.

Surprised the hell out of me when the old guy said something. "Seagull," he said. Did he say it? Or did he just make a noise? I don't know. But he leaned forward against the seat belt, pointed up and out the windshield of the car with his left hand—no question what he meant.

There was a good breeze blowing. Up above, seagulls just hung there in the airstream, white wings out, not moving a muscle. Funny how you go some-where, you see something, but don't really notice it? I suppose I'd forgotten how the seagulls hang up there so still. And *big!* These were some big birds, hovering right above us, big white wings spread out. Every now and then they moved a feather or two and changed positions. Other than that they just hung up there, sitting on that breeze like they were waiting for something. Waiting for summer to be over? Who knows?

The old guy seemed to like it, sat there in the front seat not saying a word, just looking up at them, out at the waves. I think he liked the whole beach scene— the breeze, the seagulls, the girls.

With his money, he probably had any girl he wanted, during his time. I wondered what it was like the first day you saw some really fine stuff, realized it didn't have any effect on you? Of course I didn't say anything to him about it.

When I started the car to leave, the seagulls broke formation, swooped this way and that, some diving straight at the car. The old guy got agitated, and I had to calm him down. "Hey! It's okay!" I told him. But believe me, I was spooked too.

Next time out was the Wednesday after Labor Day. We went back to the beach. The start of school wiped out the crowds, plus it suddenly cooled off. Even though it was a good day, only a few cars were scattered around the lot. The only people in the water were a couple of surfers in wet suits. There was a good surf, a pretty stiff offshore wind.

The seagulls were hanging up there again. They assume every car driving into the parking lot is eating junk food, and 90 percent of the time they're right. They eat a certain amount of shellfish, but they prefer food people leave. Which would *you* rather have, half a double cheeseburger or a couple of raw clams, full of sand? After Labor Day, when the people thin out, the food gets more scarce, and the seagulls get a little desperate. Any scrap of food and there are plenty of takers, dozens of them swooping down at once.

We pulled up to the beach, and the old guy started saying something. It caught me by surprise, he was so quiet the first two times we went out. I couldn't understand a word of it. I thought it might be about the seagulls. "Look at those suckers hanging up there, Lefty," I said, but that wasn't it. He kept talking, if you can call it that. It was more like noises than words. Sometimes sort of a moan, but not like pain, more like he was getting my attention.

For all I knew, he had to go to the bathroom, was about to have a seizure, whatever! I tried to say something to calm him down. "Good waves out there today, Lefty!" I said. I didn't know if he understood it or not, or what he understood, or if he understood anything. Still he kept up his talking. I started hearing some of the sounds repeated, though what they meant is anybody's guess. *Rrrrhhhhennigg,* he'd say. *Drremminn.*

That day there weren't more than a dozen people on the beach, mostly mothers with little kids. Almost straight ahead of us a guy was trying to get going on a sailboard, but every five yards he flopped over. I joked about it, but the old guy wasn't interested. Instead he just got louder.

I looked around the beach, wondering what to tell him, wondering what to do next. Meanwhile the old guy started moving a little in his seat. His right hand was paralyzed, but he crossed his left hand over and put it on the door handle. Then I knew.

"Hold on, Lefty!" I said. "No way!" I tried to explain we couldn't get out. "In that wind?" I said. "You see that sand blowing sideways?" He was quiet for a few seconds. "Some other day," I told him. "Some day when the weather calms down, we'll give it a shot." I figured that might not be till next summer, which was fine with me.

He seemed a little exhausted. I'm not sure if he resigned himself, or just ran out of gas. Anyway, that shut him up for the day. I would have liked to help, but you've got to draw a line. This time a dozen seagulls swooped around us as we headed out of the parking lot.

When we came back Millicent talked friendly. "Did you gentlemen have a good ride today?" Believe me, I never volunteered anything. I thought, She's so interested, let the old guy tell her.

The next Wednesday it was raining when I picked him up. He seemed pretty frail, seemed to have gotten weaker. I was a little surprised she sent the old guy out in that weather. With the rain, I knew there'd be nobody at the beach. I took him to Jamestown, out by Beavertail Light. You go right out to the rocky tip of Beavertail Point, then around the lighthouse and back. Rain and spray blew in. Even with the rain, a squadron of seagulls covered the sky around the lighthouse. You heard them screeching even over the sound of the fog horn, which went off every minute or so. Twenty-five yards out a bell buoy dinged away in the rough seas.

As we swung around the lighthouse, the old guy pointed down at the rocks thirty feet below us, slick and shiny with rain. Waves crashed in, spray flying all the way up to the windshield of the car. Crouched all over the rocks were dozens more seagulls, looking straight ahead, the weather all around them. Swear to God, some were the size of turkeys, sitting there in the rain, blinking their eyes. I wondered what *their* wingspans would be if they decided to take off. Little did I know.

I told the old guy, as a cab driver I loved rain. Let it rain a few drops, and everybody wanted a cab. "Increased revenue," I told him, in Wall Street terms. He had a few things to say about that. Nothing I understood, of course, but you could tell I got his interest. Hey, I don't mind talking Wall Street, or whatever. I've driven around some high rollers, believe me.

Coming back from Jamestown, we had a half hour left, so I got us each a Coney Island hot dog at Reba's on Spring Street. Believe me, as low as he looked, the old guy didn't need instructions on how to eat it—one-handed, too. Chomp! Chomp! I figured Coney Islands must be his favorite food. At least he went the whole time without agitating to get out of the car.

But next week he started again. By now it was getting into October, sunny but nippy, no bathing suits at the beach. There was a good wind blowing, and seagulls hung up there, waiting, facing into the wind. If a car even pulled into the lot, several would peel off, circle around. Anybody got *out* of a car, there would be dozens. In between, they hung up in the wind, waiting. Sometimes the sky down by the beach was solid seagulls.

The minute we parked, the old guy started up. It was like he wanted to talk, but when he couldn't force the words out, he just got louder. His left hand went over on the door handle. I wondered where he got the energy. You thought he wasn't going to make it from one week to the next, then he'd be full of piss and vinegar, agitating like that.

"Hold on, Lefty!" I said. I tried to think how I could reason with him. I told him I was responsible, asked him what happened if he fell. "I can't lift you," I told him. I said I probably hadn't mentioned my back, the bad disk? "The bottom line is my back," I told him. When my back was okay, I said, I'd get him out of the car, spin him all over the parking lot. "Maybe in a few weeks," I told him. It's amazing what people expect for their money, I thought. I was hired basically as a chauffeur, yet I was supposed to do miracles with the old guy.

I wondered when was the last time he went to the beach. Sometime with his wife? Maybe with his kids, too? Did he even have kids? Believe me, I was sympathetic, but I wasn't about to have a lawsuit, lose my license. Would that have made any sense? Little did I know!

He more or less calmed down after that. Without actually saying it, we came to an understanding. As long as he didn't raise hell at the beach, we could stop for a Coney Island hot dog. He loved the hot dogs, so he pretty much went along with that.

I even came to an understanding with Millicent. She trusted me, and if she had to leave a few minutes early she'd hang the keys to the car on the coatrack, have the old guy dressed and ready in his wheelchair, leave him in the front hall. The cook was always there in the kitchen if the old guy needed her, or if I was delayed. The old guy seemed to like the independence, sitting there waiting for me.

Truth is, though, he seemed to be running out of steam, practically wasting away. I don't think he weighed 110 pounds. Getting him in and out of the car, it was me did all the work. I wondered how much longer he'd be able to go out at all. Did he ever think of that? Did he realize?

At the beach I started rolling down the window on his side. He turned and closed his eyes, faced out the window.

It reminded me of my little brother, the time we went to the beach. He was only about two. We lived in East Providence, and my uncle came down from Worcester to see us. He wanted to go to the beach. It was a weekend in July, and of course there was traffic all the way down, and all the way back, and my father complained the entire trip. That man did not like to drive. Christ, I drive more in a week than that man drove his whole lifetime. Anyway, at the beach, my little brother just closed his eyes and faced straight into the wind. "He's like those seagulls," my uncle said. We all laughed.

I told the old guy about it: about living in East Providence, growing up there, about that trip to the beach. The old guy listened. Sometimes he looked straight ahead, sometimes he turned and looked out the window. Who knows what he understood, or if he understood anything? Me, I just talked. Hey, I drive a cab. People expect you to talk. Mainly, of course, I talked to keep the old guy calmed down. Let's face it, anything to keep his mind off the fact he couldn't drive his own car, couldn't take a leak without help.

Sometimes I talked to him about driving a cab, told him about fares I had. He would try to say something back. Of course I didn't understand the words, but —it's funny—I started to get the gist of what he was saying, at least whether he liked something, or didn't, whether or not he was impressed.

I told him about the New York fare. It happened one Tuesday night. I picked up my cab just after dinner, to drive the six to six. I went almost to midnight with nothing but nickel and dime fares. I knew it would be even worse from midnight to six. I was glad to have the old guy the next day, so the week wouldn't be a *complete* financial disaster.

Then, *boom!* The dispatcher called any cab in the area. A guy at the Marriott was in a hurry to go to New York City. I was just passing the tattoo parlor on Marlboro Street, so I grabbed the call. I made a U-turn, pulled up in front of the Marriott in eighteen seconds. The guy had his briefcase and a cellular phone. I got a flat rate from the dispatcher: three hundred and fifteen dollars, including turnpike and bridge tolls. The guy didn't blink an eye, just said, "Let's go." He wanted to know how quick I could get him there. I told him to fasten his seat belt and hang on.

He talked on his phone the entire time, something about a construction job in Manhattan. Believe me: *big bucks.* We flew about two feet off the ground after we got on 95, barely slowed down for the toll booths, hit the Triborough Bridge at one minute before three, were at the hotel by twelve minutes after. You should have seen those New York cabbies in front of the Sheraton Midtown wake up when Colonial Cab from Newport went to the front of the line and let the guy out. He pulled out a roll and peeled off three hundreds, a ten, and a five, for the fare. Then he peeled off an extra hundred for me. A hundred-dollar tip!

Coming back I took my time, didn't get back to Newport till 8:30 A.M. As soon as I turned my cab in, I went down to Ray's Lunch on Thames Street and ordered the #12 breakfast: sausage, eggs, pancakes, the works. By that time the regulars were already in and out. A couple of housewives were having a Danish at the end of their morning walk. I tried to tell Ray about the fare to New York, got his usual enthusiastic reaction. "Regular or decaf?" he wanted to know. Frigging Ray! You sometimes want to wave your hand in front of Ray's eyes, check if anyone's home.

I couldn't wait till that afternoon to tell the old guy. You could see he loved the story, especially the part about driving up in front of the Sheraton. You could tell he appreciated a guy going out and hustling for the extra dollar. You knew he'd done it in his time. It was like he said, *You're on the right track, Louie! You got the right idea!*

The next few Wednesdays we were getting into serious winter, but the old guy still kept going out every week. A few times I worried. How does he make it? How much longer *can* he make it?

Believe me, we talked about everything. I should say *I* talked. About the little old ladies, the rich kids. I told him about driving Anjelica Huston to the airport, about taking Jackie Kennedy's sister to the antique stores, about sneaking Robert Redford in sunglasses through the Burger King drive-up. I told him my strategy with Wanda at the Foto Stop. I ran the limo idea past him. I could tell he liked it. I knew what he was thinking, what he was trying to tell me. *Go for it, Louie!* he said. *Anything is possible!*

The last day I drove him there were a couple of extra cars in their driveway, one with Connecticut plates. On top of that the old guy was waiting for me outside, in the driveway. I was surprised Millicent left him there, because it was nippy. She had clipped gas money to his sleeve. First I thought it was the usual twenty, then realized it was a hundred. This was strange, too. With all their money, Millicent was careful, never flashed it around.

I tried to sort this out as we drove down to the beach. I was surprised how alert he was, energetic almost, ready to go. I even thought, Hey, maybe he's better. Pretty soon we were just driving along, talking, business as usual. I got to talking some more about growing up in East Providence, about high school, about my old man.

It was cloudy and windy at the beach. The old guy and I had it to ourselves, us and the seagulls. They were all over the place, even worse than usual. If possible, they seemed even *bigger* than usual. It looked like the ones from Beavertail Light had come over, like they'd come down from Maine, up from Connecticut. There must have been a colony of mussels washed up, and the seagulls swarmed all over the surf line whenever a wave receded.

I told the old guy about my little brother. He was ten when I was in high school. He always rode my bike without asking. We fought about it. He had only this dinky hand-me-down two-wheeler from one of our cousins. One day, flying out of our driveway on my bike, he got hit by a car. I came home from high school that day, saw my bike lying on its side on the front lawn. I was pissed, wanted to kill him. "Tony!" I hollered, walking into our yard. Then I saw the bike was bent up, saw people in the house, realized something had happened. I felt awful, like I caused it. Telling it to the old guy, I guess I got emotional. I'd never told anyone.

When I finished, the old guy was quiet. For the first time I could remember, he turned and looked right at me, tried to say something. I could see he understood.

Maybe that explains why I got him out. He didn't give me his noise, didn't try to put his hand on the door handle. But I thought, what the hell. "We'll get out," I told him, "but I'll still get you the hot dog." I got his wheelchair out of the trunk, folded it down for him. Some of the seagulls saw this, started ganging up overhead.

When I got the old guy into his chair, the seagulls got worse. Some of them swooped down around us. The wind was biting, and when I started to push the chair the seagulls went really crazy overhead. I was sorry I got him out, but the old guy didn't seem to mind. In fact, he looked up, tried to raise his hand toward them, even said a couple of things, like the first day we saw them. I think he enjoyed it.

Of course that's all they needed, a little encouragement. Dozens more came in out of nowhere. Hundreds of seagulls, it seemed. Big ones, too, bigger than I'd ever seen, ever imagined. When they got too close I tried to wave them away, but it was like I wasn't even there. They closed right in on us, screeching, flapping their wings all around us, especially around the old guy.

I tried to scare them off, but there was no doing it. Before I knew it, they had the old guy by the arms, lifted him right up out of the chair. Funny thing, he didn't seem to mind. He didn't say anything, didn't make his noises, didn't try to break away. He just hung on, closed his eyes, looked into the wind, let himself be carried off like that. When they got him up in the air, they all clustered around, flew away with him. Soon all you could see was a cloud of seagulls flying away. And just like that, the old guy was gone, without a peep.

My first reaction was, How did it happen? How did he do it? Then I saw his wheelchair, turned on its side and collapsed, where he had left it. And me standing there watching the whole thing like it was an air show. Can you blame me? It was something! I wanted to cheer, like a hockey game.

But I was scared, too. What would I do? Call the police? The Rescue Wagon? And tell them what? Even the Newport police wouldn't believe this story. Still, there wasn't another soul at the beach, and by then only a few puny seagulls scouring the surf line for mussels. I finally decided to take his car back. Maybe think of something along the way? I folded the chair up, put it in the trunk. Believe me, I drove twenty-five all the way back, so there was no chance of getting stopped. It was only 3:15, another forty-five minutes till Millicent was supposed to be home.

But when I got to their house, cars were parked all around the circular driveway. I had to park over to the side, by my pickup. Should I just ring the door-bell? Then what? For a minute I even thought of getting the hell out of there.

A man in a business suit answered the door, but Millicent was right behind him. "Oh, it's Louis!" she said. She introduced the guy as Mr. Winston's nephew. You could tell she'd been crying. There were people off in the sitting room, talking quietly. "We tried to call you," Millicent said. Then she broke down, motioned me inside.

The nephew took over, said Mister Winston had passed away during the night. "It was a shock to everyone," he said, "even though Uncle Bart had been fail-ing." He offered to get me a drink.

Needless to say, I wasn't anxious to stay around there. "I'm sorry," I said. "I'm sorry about Mister Winston."

Millicent cried some more and hugged me, tried to get the nephew to pay me for the week, but of course I wouldn't take anything.

It wasn't till I got home I realized I still had the keys to the old guy's car, not to mention the hundred-dollar bill. For a while I worried about how to return them, that is, without a lot of questions and so on. Finally I just put them in the drawer with my socks.

I see them there every day. I think about what the old guy told me, advice about my limo business, about life. I think about what happened.

Believe me, the hundred I'll never spend. But sometimes I wonder what would happen if one day I took those keys, went over there, took the old guy's car for one last drive. Took that sucker to the top of the Newport Bridge. And just took off. Over Jamestown, over Narragansett, over New London, over the Tri-borough Bridge. Right into the center of New York City before I even touched down, right there in front of the Sheraton Midtown, at the head of the line.

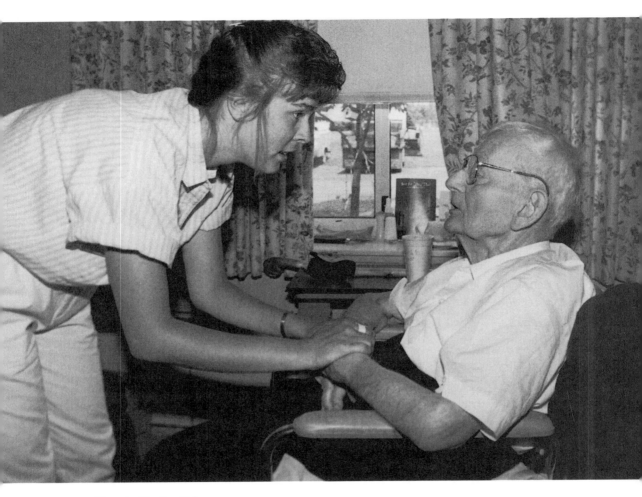

Photo by Marilyn Nolt

the oldest man in the world
Michael Strelow

Each day he does a little work in the garden,
Chases with hisses the tomcat that pees in his zinnias.
He is old, old, howling old, perishing old
But can still turn a somersault and will
If the request is from someone he knows well.
He says, "The river speaks through me," and, "I am
Older than anyone I know of. The oldest man in the world."
And, "I wear more clothes than anybody. I hate being cold."

When it rains he watches the garden from indoors, he says,
"To clear the blood. Rain clears the blood." He disappears
For days sometimes to check whether we're watching for him.
When I ring his bell, he answers, invites me in and
In a space he's cleared in the living room,
Turns a somersault unasked.

aunt hattie visits
Carol Carpenter

I find Aunt Hattie's shoe first. Right there outside my door, a pointed-toe purple shoe with rhinestones in the heel, the kind women wore in the 1960s. Almost like a warning, it stands there instead of my Saturday morning paper.

"Harry!" I shout, spotting her at the end of the hall sitting on the radiator reading the comics and chuckling to herself. I call her Harry when I'm angry, ever since that time she cashed my paycheck, boarded the wrong bus, ended up at the race track, and lost it all on some horse called Serendipity. She said if I didn't believe in serendipity, I had a lot to learn.

She hobbles toward me on one shoe, dropping newspaper pages like mulch, her Hawaiian print dress bursting into red and pink hibiscus as she gets closer.

"This slush almost ruined my best shoes. Stepped out of the cab right into a puddle," she says and bends down to pick up her abandoned shoe. "But look at that, dried good as new. Can't say I miss these Detroit winters."

Aunt Hattie winks at me as I yank her into the apartment. "Got any bacon and eggs? That stuff they serve on the plane isn't good for your digestive system." She peeks into the vestibule mirror, fluffs her pink-tinted hair, all the time peering myopically at my reflection over her shoulder.

When Aunt Hattie starts poking around in things, she stirs up a lot of dust. So I'm not about to say much, convinced I can outwait her. If it gets really bad, I can put her back on a plane. Planes leave for Florida all times of the day and night.

"You didn't say you were coming. Where's your luggage? Where's your coat?" I ask, figuring attack is better than just standing by and doing nothing. "Now I suppose we've got to go back to the airport to collect your things."

"Nope. I came unencumbered," she says, already in the kitchen cracking eggs into a bowl. "Got to thinking about that red and purple sequined dress I bought years ago at downtown Hudson's. Your mother said it was scandalous.

Cut to here," she sucks in her stomach. "Big butterfly across here," and she draws her fingers across her bosom, leaving traces of eggshell. "Need something like that for the Misty Mellow Seniors Ball next month."

"What's that got to do with anything?" Sometimes she rambles. Mother says Aunt Hattie is showing her age, even though Hattie's the younger sister. "Besides, downtown Hudson's is gone. Don't tell me you don't have stores in Miami."

"Not the kind that sell butterfly dresses. At least not around my place," she says as she flips the bacon, splashing grease that spurts up and dies away on the burner.

Over breakfast she wants to know how my night classes are going, if I ever stay after to talk to my professors, if they're all married. I tell her it's none of her business. But she won't let up. Aunt Hattie's theory is that I think too much. "Comes from reading all those books," she says. "Sometimes you just have to feel something and do it."

Right now I feel like going back to bed. After studying half the night for my computer programming class and ignoring the doorbell at seven this morning thinking it was the paperboy, I'm not very alert. In fact, it just hit me that I better call my mother before she arrives on my doorstep looking for Aunt Hattie.

Sure enough, my mother answers the phone with, "Hattie, where are you?" When she hears my voice, she starts right in telling me how Hattie is missing and how she and Charles have searched everywhere. "Even went to that martial arts center where she's been taking tae kwon do. Did I tell you she's doing that? Says she wants to cultivate her chi. Can you believe it? Says it's something to do with her internal energy." My mother sighs, and I picture her rolling her eyes like she does when she talks about Aunt Hattie. "That woman will be the death of me."

When I explain that Aunt Hattie is sitting at my kitchen table eating breakfast, my mother sighs again. "I didn't want to tell you, but the doctor says her mind may be slipping. Something about not getting enough oxygen to the brain. But they have to run some tests first." I hear her air conditioner humming in the background. "I'm sorry, dear. Just put her on the plane, and I'll meet her at this end."

I promise to keep an eye on my aunt and send her back Monday morning. My mother warns me to watch and make sure she gets on the plane. "Can't trust her to do what she says. Not if something better comes along. Never could," Mother says. I feel sad, the same kind of sadness as when the creek behind the apartment dried up last summer during the hot, dry spell. Every night when I looked out my bedroom window, all I could see was the dark riverbed; nothing moved.

Even after my mother hangs up, I hold the phone pressed against my ear, not quite ready to break the connection. I remember how when I was just a little kid, maybe ten or eleven, and stayed with Aunt Hattie, she treated me like a grownup. She took me to midnight movies and dealt me in when she played canasta with her neighbors. She even gave me a roll of nickels to bet with, and sometimes I carried my winnings in my coat pocket for a week, just to hear them clinking against each other.

Now Aunt Hattie sits at a kitchen table like she did back then, soaking up egg yolks with her toast. "I made it this long eating eggs every day. Imagine that doctor telling me I had to give up eggs. As if this is the time of life people ought to start giving up things," she complains.

I ask Aunt Hattie about this ball she's going to, wondering if she's just making it up. With her, it's often hard to tell what's real and what she just wants to happen.

"Your mother's going with Charles Bronsbottom," she says, watching to see if I recognize the name. "You really ought to talk to her about him. She won't listen to me. First thing every morning he grabs the paper to check his stocks. Tells everyone how he invested in IBM back before computers."

"Do I detect some jealousy here?" I tease.

"Of course not," she says, buttering another piece of toast. "But he's not right for her. You can tell a lot about someone by how he reads the newspaper."

I suppose she's right since I usually turn to the advice columns, reconfirming that men are more trouble than they're worth.

"You know he even insists on being called Charles. Not Charlie or Chuck. *Charles,*" she says, drawing out the syllables. "Nothing like your father, rest his soul. At least your father knew how to have a bit of fun. Didn't just stick with one boring job all his life and never complained about his arthritis like Charles," pronouncing the name "Char-less."

Aunt Hattie licks her fork, taps it on the table. "Reminds me of that James you were engaged to a few years back." She taps louder, blinking her eyes as if she's changing channels by remote control. "Humph, James. Sounds like somebody's butler. Now Brad, Rick, Mike—those are names you can sink your teeth in and hold onto. Even Johnny, a name that wraps round you like a quilt. Know any guys with those names?"

"No," I say, scrubbing harder to get the scorch marks off the frying pan. "Harry," I warn her, "life's too short to mess it up with men. Of all people, you ought to know that." Aunt Hattie's been divorced twice, engaged more times than the rings on a red cedar, and always on the lookout for what she calls good marriage material.

As she puts it, "If you want to wash windows on the second story, you have to climb the ladder." Sometimes I envy Aunt Hattie and wonder if I got cheated out of some chromosome, sort of like a computer program with code numbers reversed.

"Remember how when you were a little girl, we went to Eastern Market every Saturday?" she asks. "You used to stare into the window of the fish market. Pressed so close to the window, your breath fogged up the glass. You kept wiping the glass with tissues until everything got so smeary you couldn't see."

"That was a long time ago," I say.

"Not so long," she whispers, carrying her dirty dishes to the sink and dropping them in the water. Puddles of grease collect on the surface. "You wanted to take those fish and put them back in the lake. Never had the heart to tell you they were dead." She dumps the dishwater, turns on the tap, squirts in so much soap that bubbles erupt over the side of the dishpan and cling to her arms. A few rise toward the ceiling, popping in midair.

When Aunt Hattie decides her time's up, she'll probably just close her eyes, climb the ladder until she reaches the top, and step off, wearing her purple shoes with rhinestones.

At the back of my throat, spasms start. I gasp, scared that my throat will close off, trapping pockets of nothingness that I'll never be able to swallow. It's as if I'm standing in front of the fish market now, wondering why the ice doesn't melt.

"You had a way with you. No other little girls got to help the baker wrap the bread. While you two jabbered away, I slipped next door and bought the trout you loved so much," Aunt Hattie says. "Once they were coated in batter and cooked you never knew. Sometimes I wonder if I should have told you."

I hug her, feeling my body fit itself to her curves, kissing her cheek that tastes like the peppermint soap she uses. She grabs my hand, dripping soapsuds over my wrist, down the sleeve of my robe. "Don't ever forget who taught you to waltz," she says, placing her other hand in the small of my back and counting off the steps.

"How could I forget? And now, it's time," I announce as she dips me backward, the suddenness sending blood rushing to my head. "Let's go find the monarch of butterfly dresses."

While I'm getting dressed, I hear Aunt Hattie moving around my living room. I find her studying the stack of computer printouts I was working on last night.

"What do you do with this stuff? Looks like hieroglyphics." She lifts up the top page. The pile unfolds like an accordion.

"I debug programs," I explain as she laughs, a staccato sound as jarring as high heels against tile. "I fix the errors so the program can run."

"Seems then like you could debug your life," she says, smoothing her nylons, lamplight glinting off her rhinestone heels. "No offense, but even when you were a little girl you were afraid of lightning bugs. Always wanted me to catch them and put them in mason jars. Never could explain how some things you just can't put a lid on."

I link arms with her as I shut the door behind us. There's a small boutique I know that may carry the kind of dress she's looking for.

Aunt Hattie refuses to even try on the black, elegant dresses the saleswoman brings. "I'm not going to a funeral," she snaps as she pulls sequined dresses from the rack and holds them up to her. When she finds the one with the red rose, its stem rising from the waist, she smoothes it over her bulges.

In the dressing room, she holds her hands at her sides as I zip up the back. "Goes with my shoes," she says, fingering the purple satin skirt. "And even this small butterfly on the petal is better than none."

We tour the old neighborhood where my mother and Aunt Hattie lived before moving to Florida. The Kroger store has been torn down to make room for Blockbuster Video. Aunt Hattie's bungalow has suffered a fire and only the walls stand, waiting for the demolition crew. "It's getting rundown," I say, driving further in on familiar streets.

"Just growing into something else. That's all," she says as we spot the two-story house where I grew up. It's two-toned now, the top story yellow as the center of a daisy and the bottom forest green. Even as we watch, snow melts and runs off the roof, sinks into the frozen ground at the foundation.

"Good for tulips and crocus," Aunt Hattie says, shifting the dress box in her lap. "Wonder if those special black parrot tulips your mother planted still come up every spring."

I can almost see my mother now, on her knees, clearing away the winter debris and working rotted leaves from the compost pile into the dark soil.

Aunt Hattie says it's her treat if we stop at Carl's Chop House for a late lunch. We're seated before I remember I left my purse locked in the trunk. I'm irritated that I have to go back into the cold to retrieve it. I almost slip on a patch of ice, but catch myself on a car fender before I'm all the way down.

As my eyes readjust to the dim lights in the restaurant, I spot Aunt Hattie sitting at a different table, laughing with a man about my age and holding up her new dress. She doesn't see me moving in her direction.

She jumps slightly as I put my hand on her shoulder and quickly says, "Oh, there you are. Johnny's going to join us for lunch."

She looks back and forth between us, her eyes darting about like lightning bugs. "Really, John is his middle name, but I like it so much better than Matthew," and she folds her dress carefully before putting it in the box and setting it on the floor by her chair.

"I know someone who has a terrific dress I can borrow if you like to dance," I say.

Johnny winks at me, the same kind of wink Aunt Hattie gives when she's up to no good, the kind of wink that reminds me of a railroad crossing.

Photo by Marianne Gontarz

bloodlines
Kelly Sievers

My mother and I follow the finger
of a visiting cousin down pages
of linked lines. She straightens
stories for my mother, unfolds letters.

A great-grandfather writes:
"Dear Sir: I am sending you
the information required of all
Menominee half-breeds
who wish to be enrolled.
I am Charles Brisk son of Louis Brisk
whose mother was O-ke-mo-kiew."

From shoe boxes
stuffed with pictures,
my mother claims history.
We search for my brothers
in a blacksmith's angled arms,
a lumberjack's thick neck.
Our cousin meets
her full high cheekbones
on the face of a seamstress.
I find my mother
in my grandmother's small eyes
pulled close behind pince-nez.
An uncle poses on a pony,
my stubborn black hair pokes out
from under his cowboy hat.

There are two hundred years
that spread like a blanket
from the feet of Okemokiew.
How close we sit
on these woven strands
bumping elbows and knees.

knitting
Barbara Crooker

I

My grandmother's needles
force the soft grey yarn
into patterns old as Europe.
She came from a family of tailors,
and gave each grandchild an afghan
of her own design;
the colors glow like January fire,
the stitches are perfect,
cabled with love.

II

My mother also knits
from patterns and pictures:
mittens with snowflakes
and Fair Isle socks.
Does she weave in June days
of yellow light, the babies
quietly piling blocks, the clean smell
of steam from dampened laundry?

III

My older daughter tries to knit, too,
but her hands can't master the needles,
so she pretends and spends hours
in a tangle of wool and steel.
She is already a maker
of emperor's cloth.
See the fine patterns?
   the royal colors?
   the designs more beautiful than stars?

IV

And here I sit, like a bear in February,
huddled in yards of wool; skeined up in love,
clicking my pen across the page.
I take words and knit them back in poems.
Something could be made of this.

birthday check
Marilyn J. Boe

Aunt Lil sends me a card
folded around a check for $10,
as she has done every year
since I gave her Mother's
red wool winter coat
after the funeral.

She took it,
spoke of its warmth,
color, fit, then added,
"Of course, you understand,
I can't take charity."

In her ninety-seventh spring
she writes the check
with a shaky pen,
seals the stamped envelope,
gives it to the mailman
on the right day
to reach me
on March 14,
as it has for twenty-two years,
making this
the most expensive coat
Aunt Lil has ever owned
in her
tightly budgeted life.

Photo by Marianne Gontarz

soup for victoria
Betty Sue Fox

Thursday is our day, Victoria's and mine. Thursday has been our day to spend together for a long while now. It started when Victoria had a bladder infection resistant to antibiotics. Her first appointment was on a Thursday. The doctor wanted to check on Victoria and her medication every week and instead of taking a urine sample to the clinic, I took Victoria. I always went in with her because when the doctor would ask her how she was doing, she would say: "Oh, I'm fine. I just stopped in to say hello." And when the doctor asked about Victoria's medicine, she would say with great surprise: "Oh, I don't take any medicine. I don't need medicine for anything, you know."

And then her glasses broke. Well, really, her glasses did not break. A tractor ran over her glasses and twisted the frames and flipped out the lenses. I told Victoria that she should wear her glasses on a chain but she said no, that would make her look like an old lady. Victoria always wears her glasses on her walk because she thinks she looks better in her glasses, and when she was gathering red and orange and yellow leaves to decorate her kitchen table her glasses fell off her face onto the path that runs around the cornfield. Victoria did not notice that her glasses were gone until a neighbor, whom she could not name, delivered to her door the twisted frames and popped-out lenses. I know this is how her glasses came home because I saw one of Victoria's notes to herself that said: "Remember to write thank-you note to neighbor who drives a green Chevy with mashed-in door and found my glasses."

Victoria wore her twisted frames without the lenses and insisted that she could see as good as ever. I thought that if she could see as good as ever, then something was wrong and she should have her eyes examined but she said no, she does not need glasses and she wears them only to look better. I told Victoria that wearing the twisted frames without the lenses looked silly. Anyway, that started our Thursday trips to the eye doctor, and soon Thursdays together was a regular thing.

Victoria is my friend of my grandmother's generation, but she likes to think that we are the same age. Victoria thinks of herself as she was fifty years ago, the performer who sang and played the piano in satin off-the-shoulder gowns. Huge black-and-white photographs of her singing and playing the piano and posing with her hands about her face fill her large, open house and surround her with proof positive that she is this elegant performer. When we are out together, people sometimes ask if I am Victoria's daughter. Victoria does not like this. Sometimes she bristles a bit, and once she insisted to a bewildered clerk: "It's the other way round."

On Thursdays, Victoria and I do whatever errands need to be done. This Thursday what needed to be done was cashing checks at the bank, picking up the new glasses, having her prescription refilled, getting her hair done because she said it looks like straw and I could see a full inch of roots showing, and grocery shopping for cereal and milk and Häagen-Dazs coffee ice cream. We go to Kroger's because the bank and the drug store and the grocery are all together in the same building and they always have Häagen-Dazs coffee ice cream.

Victoria has three piano students who pay her with checks that she wads up and sticks into the hidden recesses of her paisley purse. I search out these checks and watch Victoria sign them, hand them to the bank teller for cashing, and ask in her stage whisper voice, "Would you check my balance?" After she is handed her cash and her balance is written out on a little piece of scrap paper, Victoria says, "I should put some of this back into the bank." I remind Victoria that she needs the cash for paying for the things she will be buying, and if she puts the money back into the bank she will need to write another check. When I say this, an idea strikes her as bright and new as a shiny penny and she says, in her same stage whisper to the teller, "Would you check my balance?" The teller reminds Victoria that she has just given her the balance. Victoria, astonished, looks to me to confirm her request, but I join the conspiracy against her and tell her that she has her balance as I pull her away from the teller's window.

When we go to pick up the new glasses, Victoria does not remember seeing this doctor or ordering glasses. She confuses her old broken glasses with the new ones and insists that she is not going to pay for them because she does not want them and they are perfectly ugly. She repeats over and again in her no-nonsense voice that she sees perfectly well without glasses. I tell Victoria that she has been here before and that she has already paid for her glasses and that she does need the new glasses to see. "How do you know this?" she asks with eyes wide and round, her mouth forming into a perfect red circle. "I came with you before," I say, "and the doctor said that you must have these glasses to correct your vision." And Victoria says, as she pushes the glasses away, "Well, my vision is corrected so I don't need them anymore."

At the drug store, Victoria cannot remember ever needing or ever buying or ever taking the prescription that had been refilled for her. She tried to convince the pharmacist and me, too, that there was a mistake, that she does not take medicine. The pharmacist, looking at me, repeats how much we owe for the prescription. Victoria makes a strange high-pitched sound. I pay for the medicine with money from her purse and put it in my pocket for safekeeping.

The beauty shop looks foreign to Victoria. She says she has never been to this beauty shop and, besides, she has no money. She refuses to go inside. I say, yes, you do have money and remind her that her hair looks like straw and she has to have a shampoo. "I can do that myself," she says and purses her lips and wriggles her hips deeper into the car seat. I say, "Victoria, I can see a full inch of white roots. You have to have color put on," and she unglues her bottom from the car seat, closes tightly into herself, and follows me into the beauty shop.

Our last stop is for groceries. Groceries is our last stop because the Häagen-Dazs coffee ice cream melts fast. When Victoria does errands by herself, she forgets about ice cream melting and buys it first, and when she gets home she has a chocolaty mess in her car and no ice cream for her evening snack.

Victoria spends lots of time touching and smelling and looking over the fruits and vegetables. She picks up a package of dates, flushes, flashes a flirty grin and says, "I really like the other kind of dates better." A young man catches her remark and acknowledges her presence with a puzzled smile. She pulls herself up straight, her hands flutter about her face, and her laughter sounds like her piano students playing scales.

When we are at the frozen food section, Victoria sees the bank across the store and the idea strikes for the third time, all bright and new: "I need to check my balance." I tell her no and remind her that she has checked her balance already. Her bewildered look says that she does not believe this and she asks, "How do you know?"

Victoria says that only old people make out a grocery list so she does not have one. I pull her along the aisles, pick out items I know she needs, and drop them into the cart she is pushing. She does not accept the items I put into her cart. She tells me that she does not need anything and if she does need something she will take herself to the store and get it tomorrow. "I can drive," she says. And I say, "You can drive yourself there, but you don't remember what you went for when you get there." This time, I am glad Victoria does not remember.

Victoria is exhausted from wrestling with her memory. She is shrunken and stumbly and we let the groceries go and I take her hand and lead her to the car. "Have you ever been to Brown Street Cafeteria?" she asks. This is a question, like all her questions, that she has asked often, but this time I respond differently. "Tell me about Brown Street Cafeteria," I say. She tells me that she has gone to Brown Street Cafeteria since she was a young bride and went there to meet her husband for lunch and they have good food and she wants to go to the Brown Street Cafeteria again, and in a flat, soft voice she asks: "Could we go now? I need some soup."

While Victoria has short-term memory loss, I have no sense of direction. In the fourth grade, I tell her, the class had to stand up one by one and point out the four directions: north, south, east, and west. I marveled then that it was actually possible to do this, although all my classmates could. I marvel still that anybody can.

Victoria knows direction. She knows landmarks in this place where she has lived for fifty years. It is what is happening at the moment that she does not know. She tells me what landmarks we need to find and I tell her what street we are on and, because she cannot remember, every thirty seconds she asks, "Are we on Brown Street yet?"

Brown Street is in the city, the big city. Here not only do streets angle about and go off in every direction, they change their names willy-nilly. Even if we are on Brown Street, I tell her, we might never know because it could be called another name in this section where we are.

It is really important to Victoria that we get to the Brown Street Cafeteria. Victoria melts into the car seat and worries that I will give up and we will never find Brown Street Cafeteria and she will not get soup. I promise that we will keep looking until we find it. "It" is all we know. Victoria cannot remember the name of this place. She calls it "Brown Street Cafeteria," and that is all she knows except that Brown Street Cafeteria is a wondrous place and she will know it when she sees it.

We find Brown Street. Victoria reviews her appearance in the little mirror on the back of the sun visor and adds another layer of powder to her nose and another layer of lipstick to her full red lips. I drive up and down Brown Street several times. No wondrous cafeteria. "I'm going to pull into this dumpy little place to look at the map, Victoria," I say. Victoria jumps in her seat, straightens her spine, squares her shoulders, and squeals, "This is it. We found it!"

Inside, I see a wooden floor, wobbly tables, and a food line laden with fatty, starchy foods. Victoria sees the welcome of an old home place. She holds tight to her purse and marches straight and tall past long rows of food served up in little round dishes. Victoria's right hand floats over these food items all in a row, momentarily hovering over the lima beans, the sweet potatoes, the fried cabbage, the chicken-fried steak.

We get all we want for one price. We pay $3.29 no matter what we take from the cafeteria line. Except desserts. Desserts are extra. Victoria says she is really not all that hungry and settles for soup and iced tea. I settle for dumplings and custard, which costs extra because it is dessert.

Victoria is determined to pay. At the checkout, she digs into her purse and pulls out crumpled dollar bills and numerous coins that she hands to the cashier to count. Not enough. More digging. More counting. More digging. Behind us, an old man totters against the tray line. His tray topples. His food splatters on the floor. No one acts as though this is out of the ordinary. Out come buckets and mops. The glass is swept up. The floor is wiped. The old man is shown to a table. A tray of food just like the one spilled is served him.

"Victoria, this is on me," I say, and quickly hand over a ten-dollar bill to the cashier. Victoria stops digging in her purse and looks at me with sad eyes. "I wanted to treat you," she says. I say, "Let's sit down."

We sit down. The table is wobbly. Victoria is wobbly. The soup sloshes and spills and sprinkles over Victoria. Calm waitress hands spontaneously wipe up the spills and bring new soup. Victoria rearranges herself, poising primly on her chair. The sunshine, dancing on her auburn hair, makes her a halo. Her eyes sparkle.

The custard is the best of the best. I tell Victoria this, and the thought of feeding me more lights up her face. She will pay, she says, and she calls over our waitress. The waitress responds to Victoria. I start to help. The waitress shuts me out. She turns her back to me and she faces Victoria. Victoria digs in her purse and bubbles on about her wondrous soup and how she will buy me more custard. She offers the waitress a handful of coins that her memory does not allow her to count.

The waitress collects the coins one by one with her thumb and forefinger, takes them to the cash register, returns to our table, turns her back to me, faces Victoria, and says, "I need eleven more cents, please." Victoria glows, ceremoniously digs into her purse, and comes out with a quarter that she offers to the waitress on her open palm. The waitress approves Victoria's offering, solemnly picks it from her palm, carries it to the cash register, returns to our table, turns her back to me, faces Victoria, and says, "I had this change left over from the money you paid for the custard."

Victoria is jubilant. She holds out her right hand, palm up, fingers extended, and takes her change. Her fingers wind around the coins and she grips tightly, forming a fist. She beats the air with this fist full of coins and triumphantly tells me, "I can treat you!" I am warmed by her radiance. I say, "Yes. Yes you can," and her sunshine spills all over me.

bread and roses
Susan Jacobson

You learn a lot of things
in this job, for instance
to take flowers to a woman
who hasn't walked in years,
whose diapers and socks
are never changed, who
hasn't any food, who
has a large teddy bear
frequently speckled
with fecal matter (hers),
a floor likewise (her cat's),
who is often left alone at night
in the dark, except for
her plastic Madonna night-light,
to take flowers to this woman
is stupid, elitist, asinine.

You learn, you learn—
such questions as
You married? Got kids?
mean *Do you know what you're doing?*
Will you be gentle with me? and
How long you stay? You come back?
mean *I trust you.*
You learn not to speak to her
of what you are seeing, hearing—
words would make it real, unbearable.
You commune with your eyes,
make a rosary of touch,
a litany of routine.

You leave your flowers in the garden
to seed themselves for next year,
take yogurt and oatmeal, instead.

You learn that rage
is a defense mechanism.
It doesn't help you
to walk into that house each morning,
but it is infinitely easier than
documenting what you find there,
writing the dispassionate prose
one impotent word after another:
   . . . lying supine with lower body
twisted to the right . . . I again
requested that the family . . .
urine with a strong smell of
ammonia saturating the sheets . . .

It is far more sensible
to take food to this woman.
It is appropriate behavior.
Until one morning you find her
with two wilted roses in her hand,
her body curled around them
and her other treasures (her glasses,
an empty cosmetic bag, her plastic watch),
until you hear her say *I find, I find*
with the defiance and delight
of a three year old, refusing to let go,
and you learn that fragrance, fragility, beauty
are bread for the hand, the eyes, the heart.

Photo by Sharon Gurman Socol

she who holds the mirror
Joyce Lombard

Rachel greets me this spring day,
short grey hair frees fiery earrings.

Now on the shady side of eighty
she buried her husband of fifty-nine years
three days after they painted the kitchen.
That's when she said:
My life as I've known it is over,
and she sorted and pruned
and four years later acquired a boyfriend.

> *I remember sultry summers,*
> *how we'd sit at the emptied table*
> *long after the floor was mopped,*
> *how she seemed revived by the longings*
> *of this thirteen-year-old niece whose parents*
> *had grown weary. I left her papered walls*
> *with hope intact—carried her into my life*
> *as a needed rib.*

Rachel tells me she has an apartment
that harbors no peach trees,
no husband's socks for mending.
Readying to move, she brought in
eight grandchildren to pick their favorites
from her travel treasures.

With a smile in her eyes she says:
There's little time to dust.

sounds
Elisavietta Ritchie

Great-aunt Eleanora is giving us trouble these days. She wants to stay on her ramshackle farm. Alone.

"You can't even get good TV here!" argues the realtor, urging her to listen to a certain developer who'll carve the farm into twenty-nine waterfront lots.

Reception is haphazard only because the house is down on the river.

Great-aunt Eleanora has no time for television. Radio provides her news and good music. She listens as she paints—currently, murals. She started on murals when she had to stay within earshot of Great-uncle Ramsey and after thirty years could no longer hide out in the chicken coop, which Ben had helped her convert to her studio. There, she painted what she wanted, and when Ramsey was out, shipped the canvases off to a gallery in New York. Ben, and later I, transported the bigger paintings in the farm truck. Her works sold slowly over the years, but we quietly invested the proceeds in a fund that now pays the taxes on the farm. So no need to sell it.

I'm one of the few people who knows this. She assigned me power of attorney.

Though now from the rafters a family of black turkey vultures would observe every stroke of her brush, she talks of working in the chicken house again, "once the weather warms and these darn murals are finished."

Today she shows me the half-painted walls in the front hall.

"Still some baffling blanks, and the moats look empty. Ramsey suggested lotus and Ben urged lilies—but it's old-ladyish to paint flowers. Last week a stag walked through the snowy yard, then obliged me by standing still—downright posing—under the English walnut while I sketched him onto that panel between the windows. But horses I need to study live again."

The murals are medieval scenes of knights and their ladies galloping or strolling around various picturesque European hillsides. Frankly, they aren't particularly well-executed, proportions are off, not half as good as her earlier impressionistic paysages, seascapes, and passionate abstracts.

But Great-uncle Ramsey Leigh hates abstracts. A retired judge, he likes historic scenes and would wheel his chair, with Ben wheeling along in his wake, into whatever room she was painting. The fact that her eyesight and her hands were no longer as sure didn't matter to them: their own eyesight and coordination were failing. That didn't stop them from advising.

Increasingly, Great-aunt Eleanora cared for both old men, one white, one black. Ben's grandson Percival and I shoved the dining table against the wall and moved in their beds, so they'd be easier to feed and keep an eye on while she was in the kitchen. On bright winter days, the sunporch heated up so they could all nap out there.

Then, even with Percy's help bathing and lifting them, it got too much for Great-aunt Eleanora. Or so the county social worker insisted: "Judge Leigh and that old Ben are two big heavy men, and here you are, a little wren, trying to care for them day and night!"

A private room came available for Great-uncle Ramsey at the Home, and for Ben a bed in the ward.

I thought we'd have a time persuading them to move. But they consulted each other, just as they used to consult over the no-till way to sow soybeans while harvesting winter wheat, and did the barn need a new roof, the horse a new shoe. Finally they agreed to visit the Home: each had cronies there already, hadn't seen them for ages. They let us sign them in.

"For one week," Uncle Ramsey said. "But just shove us both into the same room: that'll be cheaper, and we smoke the same brand of tobacco."

The admissions secretary blinked, but Aunt Eleanora and I okayed it so the matter was arranged.

Turns out, Uncle Ramsey and Ben rather like being sweet-talked by those pretty nurses, the large-screen color television beats the old black-and-white set at the farm, and though old ladies complain, in the common room they can smoke without Aunt Eleanora coughing. Still, away from familiar surroundings, they've grown increasingly confused.

At home, though her eyesight is blurring, Aunt Eleanora continues to extend her murals throughout the downstairs. Cats brush against wet paint, leaving her pictures fuzzy and their tails purple and green. I wash the cats and her hair with turpentine and baby shampoo, just as she used to wash mine when I was a child. While my hair was drying in the sun, she would teach me to read from a tiny maroon-covered primer, and how to sculpt and fire the ungainly statuettes that remain aligned on an upstairs shelf like awkward anchors for my soul. While we shelled peas, baked cakes, or washed dishes together, she would tell me stories, usually about the great dead artists.

Now she sometimes tells them aloud to herself as she cooks what she needs to feed herself and twenty-six (at last count) cats. The farmer who's leased the fields cuts fallen branches into logs small enough for her to put in the old stove. He also plows her road after snows, and Wednesdays his wife brings groceries. I come by most weekends with a cake or casserole to last several days. Since her washing machine rusted through, I do her laundry in town. I lug my computer to catch up on my cases and to manage her bills and the correspondence that still comes in from galleries and other artists. I also bring new brushes and paints, and sometimes, friends for a picnic. She prefers young people.

At her request, every visit I check on every inch of the farm, attempt to patch whatever needs patching. During my childhood summers here, Ben used to let Percy and me tag along to "help," soon taught us to work with wrench and saw, tractor and scythe. So last week Percy and I shored up the sunporch, but another board's always rotten somewhere. The roof leaks into the upstairs bedrooms, though since she's had trouble with steps, Aunt Eleanora now sleeps off the kitchen, where Ben lived until his legs gave out. In winter the dinosaur furnace tends to die, or the chimney gets blocked as when thirteen bricks fell into the flue, and the sweep also removed thirteen buckets of soot. The electricity fails in storms, the circulating pump breaks, the septic tank . . .

More than one midnight I've driven from the city at sixty-five miles per hour to cope. And some night, it will be that Aunt Eleanora has tripped over a cat and broken a hip, or wandered to the beach and waded in too far. So of course I'm concerned about her, out here all alone now, fields on three sides, the river on the fourth.

"Just sell the place," people urge, "move her into the Home, and you won't have any more worries."

Since I am her closest relative, everyone is pressuring me. Sometimes I'm tempted. A terrible decision, to wrest her from her beloved riverside farm. Today I bring up the move.

"I am perfectly fine *here,* thank you."

January's wind methodically flaps the shed roof, beats magnolia boughs against the house, rattles windows—three panes slipped from their sashes as the putty crumbled, and the glazier is always coming *next* week. Cats meow to enter or exit, I suspect some other animal in the cellar, the forgotten teakettle shrills; even the chicken soup I'm cooking makes unearthly burbles.

"But don't all the odd noises bother you at night?"

"At night," she shrugs, "of course there are sounds. Most I identify: from the woods, the hoot owl. From the cove, loons. Scratchings, shrills, chirps in the roof, wind spiraling down all three chimneys—each has a singular moan. And when I pry rot from a window frame, the squeal that freezes against the pane is explainable."

Since Aunt Eleanora is much alone, whenever she has company, she really talks.

"But . . . " She pauses to pour hot water into the pot, not noticing it splash on the worn Oriental rug. "It's the *voices* the farm has absorbed across three hundred years—just imagine, from Indian plaints to colonial cries of love! Then this morning when I looked out the kitchen door to see if you had arrived, I noticed among the spindly figs and runaway vines covering the foundations of that shack burned in the Revolution—who knows which side lighted the torch—I noticed a child in a dark pink pinafore."

"What child?" The nearest house is a mile away, no children there. No picnickers land on her beach in January.

"A child . . . plump, about three. She was crying, her nose was running, she had a cold, or was cold. Then, she was *gone* . . . Or, was never there."

"Perhaps not."

"But every spring when the garden is plowed, in a near furrow—remember that broken pipe that leads to the barn?—always I find one tattered rag doll. You might check in the pony cart."

Except for Ramsey's ancient Packard and the farmer's tractor, the barn has stood empty for years. But the wood is good, and the stalls still bear the names of horses I learned to ride on: "Smokey," "Storm King," "Old Jess."

Could raise horses again, someday . . .

Absently cradling an orange kitten named Titian, Aunt Eleanora stares toward the river. Can she see two black vultures in the moribund oak?

I pour tea into chipped china cups. "But aren't you ever afraid here?"

"Of . . . ghosts? Nonsense. I early learned to settle in with presences. As with the woodchucks in the cellar, raccoons in the roof, cats in the barn, their ancestors guard. In time," she smiles, "my voices too will merge with the farm."

"Voices? Did you discuss this with the doctor?"

"This?" She looks puzzled. "The . . . voices? Whatever for? And it's not always voices. Mostly, it's like your computer pinging even if the power's off, or high-tension lines humming across the fields in a blizzard."

"Ringing in the ears can mean something's wrong."

"I meant to mention it to the doctor last week. Happens whenever I close my eyes. A hive in the brain." Her blue eyes focus on me. "You must hear them too. In town, there's always an ambulance down the avenue, fire engines across the park, jackhammers, traffic, that school yard six blocks away, hooves striking cobblestones."

"Except the cobblestones were asphalted over years ago, and there aren't horses in town anymore."

"Sounds pile up, you know, are stored. Volcanoes that exploded decades ago remain in the air. Cathedral chimes, troubadours' chants, street cries. High-pitched notes that set dogs howling. That's what I hear, when I wake in the night or try to nap after lunch. A music box under my pillow, roosters behind the drapes. I wonder, has my skull become one vast receptor . . . "

Suddenly she looks troubled. "Do I also transmit?"

"Transmit?" The social worker may well be correct: incipient senility.

"I certainly don't generate. I doze in the armchair—no creaky rocker for me—radio off, phone off the hook. My necklaces that used to tinkle and jangle—I moved like a belled goat—have been stolen. Or sold?"

"You gave them all to me, Aunt Eleanora, don't you remember? One every birthday for the last twenty years. But I'll return them, you obviously miss them, I don't need more than one."

Once she goes into the Home, any jewelry will disappear.

"Oh, don't worry about returning those baubles, dear. I can still hear their symphonies on my bare neck. Lovely . . . Yes, the doctor suggested tests my next checkup, next year. Today," she looks radiant, "today I'm tuned to a fishmonger's serenade . . . Now it's whistling swans. And sometimes, from farther waters, choirs of whales."

She settles back in her armchair. Leonardo, the piebald tomcat, jumps onto her lap. She is content with her voices, her cats. And glad for my company once a week.

Then she jumps up, spilling Leonardo and her untouched tea, gathers her splattered smock from its hook, her palette and paints from the kitchen.

"*Swans*—that's what I need for the moats. And a whale for the bay beyond. Would you mind shining that light there—just bend its neck—so I can see what I'm doing. Almost out of white paint—could I trouble you to bring me a tube next week?"

I jot *white paint* in my notebook. I'm forgetful of late; if I don't write down—

"Now, child, I don't want to detain you. You have a long drive, your job tomorrow. Take those cookies for the road. There, in the Louis Sherry tin."

I look in the pantry. The tin, among shoe boxes marked ZIPPERS, FUSES (BLOWN), OLD SHADE PULLS, SHEEP SKULLS, ARROWHEADS, is empty. I write *Fig Newtons* on my list. When I was six, she taught me to arrange them into castles and battlements, as if they were dominos.

Given how the cats are scratching, I add *flea powder.*

In the corner of the kitchen I notice a paper bag full of bread crusts. For the ducks. Although the weather has been too cold for her to venture outside, she still intends to go down to the inlet with the crusts. Despite the cats, there is evidence mice are taking their share on the way. She won' t let me buy traps or poison.

Knowing I must be visiting, the social worker phones.

"Good news! Your aunt finally leads the waiting list for the Home. Could be a matter of only a week, at worst two, before . . . "

Before another resident dies and frees up a bed. Before we—I—must face packing her up. Just the essentials that might survive institutional laundering. The rest—when I've gotten around to cleaning her closets and drawers—will be bagged for Goodwill: button shoes, long silk dresses, splattered smocks. As she says, Always someone out there might find a use. The stained rugs, split mattresses, and fractured chairs will go to the dump. What of her half-finished canvases stacked in the chicken house?

"How's your aunt doing?" the social worker asks cheerily.

"Great," I answer. "Let's let her stay here a bit longer. Someone else in more desperate need for a bed can take her place. If necessary, I can get leave from work for a few weeks to care for her here."

Even years . . . Since I'm supposed to inherit this farm, *I'd* better get used to staying here in season and out. Until one morning they discover *me* collapsed in the barn, or drowned on the beach, or shriveled and stiff in this wildly painted parlor, even with brushes dried in my hands. That's the way to go, Aunt Eleanora has said.

I thank the social worker, hang up.

"Next weekend," I promise Aunt Eleanora, "rain or shine, I'll drive you around to see horses. And if the weather should be warm—it *will* be spring soon—I'll walk you down to the cove, and we'll feed some crusts to the ducks. I could even push you in a wheelchair all the way up the path to the lighthouse."

Preoccupied with outlining her swans, she seems not to pay attention.

I tape another sheet of plastic over the broken panes, then bank the fire, raise the thermostat, go outside with a broomstick to check the level of heating oil. Enough to last till April. Afraid she'll forget the chicken on the stove, I cut the flame: she doesn't mind lukewarm soup. I wash and refill the dishes of the anxious cats. What would happen to them?

Despite the cold, I run to the cove with the bag of crusts. Mallards swim around the far side of a broken skiff caught in the ice rimming the shore. Waves are sparkling between ice floes.

"Here you are!" I fling the crusts: they skid across the ice toward the open water where the ducks retrieve them greedily. "More crusts next week, I promise you."

I jog along the little beach. Around the bend, suddenly twenty swans fly in line; they fracture the sun, then veer so low their feet and wing tips skim the water like skipping stones. One swan breaks formation, swerves off from the others, lands in the cove. At last the rest follow.

When I stop in the house to gather up my computer and Aunt Eleanora's laundry, I hear her humming. She is painting a whale into a cove between the tall clock and the fireplace.

The whole drive to town, the humming persists.

the dowser at eighty-five
William J. Higginson

Her salt-and-pepper hair
was pulled back in a bun.
Her hands lay still
on the faded apron in her lap
as she spoke of finding water,
of how, when she was a girl
on the farm just across the road,
neighbors used to send for her
to come and tell them
where to dig the well.

"You don't believe me."
I couldn't convince her that I did,
so I followed her outside
where she snapped a young branch
from a tree in the yard
and quickly stripped off
its leaves and smaller twigs,
leaving a lopsided, short-stemmed fork.
Taking one tine in each hand
she pointed the butt end to the sky
and started slowly walking
along the path beside the house.

We both knew the water table was high,
here only a few yards from the brook.
That was not the point.
The point of that crotched branch soon shook
with slow vibrations like a low-pitched tuning fork.
And then it began to bend, still shaking,
and point outward, then down toward the ground,

still vibrating like the floating needle
of a gigantic compass, irresistibly
twisting the branch practically out of her hand.

Sweat stood out on her forehead
as she muttered, "I couldn't *make* it do that . . . "

When the trembling stick nearly bent double
she let go one tine and it snapped back
to a right angle, then more slowly
toward its original shape.
She held the palms of her hands for me to see
how red, how raw they were from holding that stick
against the power neither of us understood.
And tears filled her eyes—
"You see?"

c e n t e n a r i a n

Susanne E. Moon

Eyes
that reflect a century
or more
greet me in the predawn
as we struggle
together
to maintain
the dignity of a lifetime.
This body
housing a richness
of soul
and experience
guessed at by few,
has walked through history.
Memories shine
through mists of confusion
like a lighthouse beam
piercing the fog.
We steer
toward the pleasant beaches
of content—
away from the rocky coast
of anger
humiliation
and loss.
Together
we struggle
to preserve
the dignity of a lifetime.

Photo by Marianne Gontarz

her century
Scott Lipanovich

In the towns of coastal northern California you still meet immigrants who arrived in the early part of this century. Most came via Ellis Island and cross-country train trips. They often live in the same houses where they raised their children, the interior walls and wood floors—even their accents—largely unchanged for fifty, sixty, seventy years.

In Sonoma County, where I come from, the most numerous of these immigrants are Russians and Italians. They talk about Mussolini, Stalin, or the Bank of Italy in the same earnest tones our parents speak of Pearl Harbor and the W.P.A. They live on savings and social security. Their children, now middle-aged or seniors themselves, scattered during the great economic expansion that followed the Second World War. Put simply, they moved to suburbs and made more money than their parents ever dreamed of. Their parents—the old people I write of—stayed with their vegetable gardens and apple trees. They stayed where their long journeys had deposited them.

One by one they die. Each has a story. This past year we lost Gemma Accomazzo, who was ninety-eight. Time and weather had grooved her face, toughened her skin, yet the passing of this century had made her beautiful. Her eyes were hazel, clear and fiery. Her white hair was always held back neatly in a clip. Five feet tall and a hundred pounds, whenever she worked you saw gnarled muscles jump along her arm.

Although her clothes were often dirty and her tennis shoes muddy, Gemma carried herself with a nimble, singular grace. Through her eighties, at family wedding receptions, a moment came when the band stopped and the dance floor was cleared. Then Gemma glided to the middle, a glass of water balanced on her head. A nephew or grandson was pushed into the ring with her. The band played a slow song while Gemma and her partner joined hands and circled the floor. When the song ended, she presented the glass to the young man. He would raise it. Amid raucous applause he would drink it down. The celebration was thus kicked into high gear.

Gemma and her husband, Paul Accomazzo, traveled from Italy to California in 1913. Gemma was sixteen. They borrowed money from friends and bought a three-room cabin on forty-five acres. The price was two thousand dollars. The land was steep, rocky, brushy. Gemma and Paul cleared the land and made it bloom.

For years they grew or shot all of their food. To earn cash Paul trapped raccoons, squirrels, and rabbits. The pelts were sold on Sundays, when the young couple took their wagon on a two-hour trip to Guerneville. As another source of income, Gemma picked grapes for Korbel, and prunes on ranches near the then tiny town of Healdsburg. She nursed three babies in the fields.

Fifty years later my wife and I lived near Gemma, on a ridge a mile above the Russian River. We didn't have a TV, but she did, and most nights the three of us spent an hour or two together watching the news. Her education wouldn't have graduated her from junior high school; however, Gemma rarely failed to provide a refreshing view of a politician or current event.

She was a hell of a good cook, she made red wine, and she embroidered stunning white tablecloths, but what made Gemma interesting to us was her passion for politics. Her mind was feverish with breaking news. You could hardly say hello before she would hand you a newspaper, point to an article, and say, "What do you think?" She would nod while you read and gave an opinion. Then she would wave a finger and say, "This is where you're wrong."

During the years we knew Gemma, her husband long dead, she worked outdoors every day and generally got things put away in time for the six o'clock news. We watched a black-and-white set that was connected to an antenna strapped to a Monterey pine a hundred feet uphill from the house.

Gemma's was a physical life, and this dominance of the physical over the intellectual extended into how she reacted to politicians. She would echo their expressions: smile, frown, shake her head, lean forward and wave a hand. To glance from the TV to Gemma imitating someone on the screen gave you a different, often insightful, take on what the speaker was up to. And she would repeat his or her words aloud. I think she did this to help with her continual translation between English and Italian. Coming from Gemma, rather than a well-groomed politico, the jargon and catchy phrases were stripped of their appeal. Their fundamental emptiness was revealed.

Even more powerful than her comments on public affairs was Gemma's kindness. If tragedy struck anyone in the hills around us, she sent homemade bread and ravioli. If someone lost their job, she reached into her stash and offered that person crumpled dollar bills. She labored for days over a note she sent to Jimmy Carter after his mother died.

One by one they die. My kids will never really get to know old Russians and Italians, will probably never see a ninety-year-old woman circle the dance floor with a glass of water on her head. And as politicians come and go, and pundits and newscasters try to tell us what it all means, I miss Gemma's common sense.

A few years ago a friend of mine returned from a trip to Italy. He wanted to visit Gemma so he could speak Italian with her. During their conversation, my friend asked Gemma what had made the greatest impression on her over the course of her life. He reminded her that she had lived through two world wars, had seen the triumph of the automobile, air travel, and the development of computers, had watched a man walk on the moon.

As always, Gemma nodded thoughtfully, thinking things through. Then she spoke rapidly, passionately, about food, weather, and people. Nothing else.

thank heaven for little girls
Ann Elizabeth Dekorsi

"Ach du lieber, the back! Keep the chin up! Why do you bend the knees? You will never be dancers! Look at you in the mirror!"

I sat behind the curtain separating the practice room from the reception area and half-heard professor Helmut Lieber's critical monologue. Listening to him, you'd think the girls in his ballet class were all hand-picked klutzes, hopeless urchins attempting to become dancers.

I pulled my sweater tightly around me in the damp, drafty basement that was his studio, office, and occasional recital hall. I glanced up from my needle-point canvas when another mother called my name.

"Yes," I said, turning to face the woman next to me.

"Does he always talk to them like that? My daughter hasn't wanted to come for the last couple of weeks, and I came to find out why. Now I think I know."

My immediate reaction was to defend this hunchbacked, white-haired little man with his white ballet slippers and ridiculous polka-dot bow tie.

"I imagine at seventy-two, one's patience with little girls is somewhat strained," I replied. "He is an excellent instructor. Andrea has been with him for two years, and Kati this last year."

"Aren't they afraid of him?"

"No; Andrea laughs at him. And Kati ignores him for the most part. It shows in her dancing. I suspect a sensitive child would have problems, though."

"Yes, my daughter is sensitive. I'm sure I'll have to put her into another school after the Christmas recital."

Ah, yes, I thought, the Christmas recital. The Professor, as he liked to be called, was especially tense because this annual recital was his vehicle to show his talents as a dancer and instructor to the rest of the world, even

Photo by Marianne Gontarz

though that world consisted of the relatives and friends of his students and whoever else could be coaxed into buying a ticket in this small community.

This group, however, was inflated by the Professor's numerous friends. Their loyalty always surprised me because he was such a blunt, conceited little tyrant at times. But hadn't I also just defended him?

I heard crying behind the curtain and the Professor, in a soothing voice, saying, "Ach, it will all be better by the time you get married."

Almost immediately, he pivoted around the curtain with a little girl by the arm.

"Mrs.," he said, turning to the woman seated next to me, "you take her home. She is fine but she cries all the time, and the other students have much work before the recital."

"Mrs. Hoffman," the Professor continued, looking me straight in the eye, "Kati will never be a dancer. She has no coordination. She will carry the cue cards during the recital." He pivoted and disappeared behind the curtain.

I shook my head and my eyes rested once again on a blown-up poster of the Professor dancing as a young man. He had told me once that he had been a dancer with the Royal Ballet Company. It was hard to picture this old man as the handsome, poised dancer in the poster, although the features were there: the bushy eyebrows, the too-large nose, and the sensuous mouth. And then, of course, there were those eyes—those piercing blue eyes that at one moment seemed to mock you and the next to soften into pools of water.

The sadness I saw at those moments made me so uncomfortable that I would have to turn away so as not to let him see my pity.

He certainly didn't want pity, and why should he? The Rotary Club requested him as a speaker, as did the Toastmasters Club. His culinary delights were widely known, and he often made all the appetizers and pastries for local parties. This was in addition to teaching cooking classes in the summer during the ballet school's recess, and choreographing high school plays.

The class was over and I rose to avoid the stampede. As the girls scurried to get coats, hats, mittens, I glanced at the Professor standing by the cookie jar. He looked weary but smiled and offered each girl a cookie and a pat on the head.

I noticed there was another stack of ballet albums, priced for sale, on his desk. Lately, he seemed to be selling everything he owned. I purchased a few cookbooks the week before, and we certainly didn't need any more ballet albums. I walked over and went through them anyway.

"This one is good for Andrea," he said, as he sneaked up behind me.

"Yes," I reluctantly agreed. "I'll take it."

I always felt guilty about the measly amount I paid him every month for the girls' lessons, but then no one else paid him any more. It was what had attracted me to the school in the first place.

"Professor, maybe you should raise your tuition," I said, avoiding his eyes. "All the other schools in the area are charging more."

"Ach, no. What do I need money for at my age? I might lose some of my little girls if I do this."

Impulsively, I invited him to dinner over the Christmas holidays. Instead of accepting eagerly, he said he would have to get his appointment book. I watched as he checked the weeks before and after Christmas and was surprised to see that most of the boxes were filled in—all except for Christmas day.

"Christmas is fine," I said quickly before I had time to change my mind. I already had a full house for dinner.

"That will be fine," he answered, "but you have to pick me up. I don't drive, you know."

"No problem," I said, wondering how I was going to manage that with cooking and guests.

"By the way, Professor, the girls would like to know what you want for Christmas."

"I need some warm slippers. My apartment is cold, and my ballet slippers are not warm enough anymore. I must be getting old," he said with a twinkle in his eye.

The next week was absolute chaos at the dance studio. Because of Christmas vacation, practices for the recital were scheduled every day. More mothers threatened to take their girls out of the school.

"What does he expect?" one said to me. "These are children, not professionals."

I didn't answer but quietly observed him as he demanded perfection then lovingly praised the children when he knew they had given him their best.

Andrea was a joy to watch. Her long legs and graceful body were firm and straight, and she held her head high. Her blond hair, coiled tightly in a bun, and her peach complexion gave me the impression of a small, perfect tree that knew it would one day be majestic. She had told me the Professor had taken her hand and said that some day, if she worked hard, she might become a prima ballerina. "Mom, he had tears in his eyes."

The night before the recital, he walked in with a cane. The girls scrambled around him, asking what had happened.

"I slipped on ice. Don't worry and get to work."

That night, he used the cane to tap a few of their bent legs. I was angry and left quickly after the rehearsal.

"Thank heaven for little girls, for little girls, for little girls grow up in the most delightful way. Thank heaven for little girls . . . "

The Professor's cane tapped lightly on the stage as he walked around the little girls seated at his feet. His song ended the recital, and he received a standing ovation. He tossed the cane aside, took a deep bow, and walked proudly off the stage.

A reporter from the local newspaper came up to him and asked how he managed all this at his age. The Professor laughed and said, "At twenty-seven, one can do anything."

"Isn't that seventy-two, Professor?"

"That's what I said, twenty-seven."

He wouldn't, however, let the reporter get away with only those few words to print.

"Here's my secret," he quickly added. "From the fountain of youth, you catch life. If you go around like this," he stooped over, hobbling as with the cane, "you won't last too long. But if you go with the young folk," he spread his arms and almost leaped, "they give you their life and spirit. And out of their life, you get yours.

"I get my life from my little girls."

Christmas day dawned brightly. I had set the alarm early so I could finish the preparations for dinner and have time to pick up the Professor. As I later drove down the nearly deserted country roads, the whiteness and stillness of the day put me in a daze. I felt alone in the world and then thought of how the Professor must feel, having dinner with a family he knew only on a professional basis, on a day as special as this one.

I parked my car as close to his apartment as possible to avoid having him walk the icy path and also to save him, and myself, the embarrassment of having to catch him should he fall again.

I rang his doorbell and it was quickly answered by the small, grinning man. He was dressed in a suit, vest, and his usual polka-dot bow tie.

I suppressed a laugh, and said, "Merry Christmas, Professor."

"Merry Christmas to you, my dear. I just have to get my coat and we can be on our way."

His coat was a black cloak to match his black suit, and he topped that off with a black cap with a visor. I envisioned the faces of my relatives when I brought this strange little man home.

He handed me a large cardboard box and said it was for me. He said he'd carry two smaller, brightly gift-wrapped packages. So much for holding on to him, I thought, as we walked out the door to the car.

The ride home was strained as we attempted to make small talk. When we were almost home, he told me he didn't drive anymore, but proudly noted that he still had his driver's license. "I had an accident five years ago and was thrown through the windshield," he whispered. "That is why my back is no longer straight. I am thankful every day that I did not hurt anyone else."

We fell silent as the day outside, and I was relieved that there were fifteen others at home to keep the ball rolling.

Safely inside our home, he greeted everyone warmly. He presented the two small packages to my daughters.

"You wait until after we eat to open them," he told the girls firmly. Then he told me to open the large cardboard box, making the girls pout at my good fortune.

I lifted out of the box the most beautiful and intricate gingerbread house I had ever seen. He had stayed up late every night since the recital to bake, frost, and decorate this masterpiece. It was partially covered with white frosting, gumdrops, cookies, and candy canes. The shutters and fence were pretzels cemented down with more frosting to resemble snow, and tiny plastic elves surrounded the structure.

"This is your centerpiece," he said proudly.

I was speechless but managed to wave to my mother in the dining room to dispose of the centerpiece already there. I thanked and hugged him, surprised that his slight frame was by no means fragile.

Throughout the meal, he kept everyone amused and enthralled with his stories. He laughed, ate, and drank wine. Everyone loved him, especially Andrea, who sat next to him and was the recipient of an occasional pat on the head.

My mother-in-law asked him why he continued to work so hard at his age. "Twenty-seven is not old," he replied with the familiar twinkle in his eyes. "I love my dance, I love little girls."

I shifted uneasily in my chair as my mother-in-law eyed him suspiciously. He looked her straight in the eyes. "My daughter—she was killed by the Nazis. It is a sad, sad memory, but I continue to teach little girls because I could never teach my Lisa. I do it for her and I do it for all my little girls."

Andrea looked stricken. The rest of us sat in silence. Suddenly, he clapped his hands and said, "This was long ago, today we celebrate.

"A fiddler on the roof?" he said loudly. "Sounds crazy, no?" Before our eyes, he turned into Tevye, a Jewish peasant, singing the opening song of the musical. He grabbed Andrea and began to dance.

the dance teacher
at the senior center

Charles Harper Webb

waltzes, weaves and pirouettes
among the men, urging them on:

Bill, with his bald head; Bob, whose white
beard can't hide a pea-sized chin;

Stu, with glasses and a veiny nose;
Chuck, with his dachshund legs;

Vince, his gorilla gut. "Come on, dance
with me! Come on you guys, let's go!"

While the hi-fi wheezes tired disco,
Susan of the Bolshoi body and the Botticelli

smile moves among them like a breeze
cooling cornstalks after harvest,

like rain on ancient grapevines,
its soft fingers blessing every one.

the damaged heart
Katherine Govier

Morris was pink, and this was unusual. For the past decade and a half, he had been grey. Grey of complexion, grey of humor, his hair past recall of its former black, his skin grooved, and his eyes pouched, as if they had seen too much.

But now he was energetic; there was a lift in his gaze and his rosy lips moved constantly, making words, smiling, tasting. The reason for Morris's (Mo for short, Mao to certain youthful colleagues) improved health was simple. He had a new heart.

By the time the transplant came he had given up, actually. His wife had died. His niece, Flo, thought he'd been on the list too long; he'd never get one now. Doctors liked to give hearts to people who had years to go. And even if now, at his age, a heart came his way, the operation itself would be a risk.

As nearest relation, Flo had got the call.

"We have a heart," said the careful female voice at the other end of the telephone line. "If he wants it."

"He'll want it."

"Before he says yes, there are some things you should know." Flo listened. What she heard was that this was the heart of a seventeen-year-old girl. Along with three other teenagers she had been killed in a four-car collision on Highways 400 and 88 at three o'clock that morning.

"Oh," said Flo.

"It's not a perfect heart. There's been some . . . damage."

"Otherwise, why him," said Flo.

There was a tactful pause. The person in charge of intake hadn't heard that. Then with a note—pride? very faint umbrage?—she said, "Frankly, he's not our first call."

"Meaning?"

"Meaning several people have rejected it already."

"Who?"

"Younger people in need of a heart, who can afford to wait."

"Of course."

"The girl had rheumatic fever as a child. And then there was trauma in the accident. She didn't die immediately; her injuries put a strain on the organ," the woman continued.

All Flo got out of that was the word *organ*. It sounded awfully personal: he was her uncle, after all. She continued to listen. The details of the damage were too complex for Flo to digest at that moment, but she understood that with any luck this heart could beat on for a good decade. She stammered her assurances that yes, they should call Morris, and no doubt he would want it.

The phone rang on the morning of a cold, clear November day. Morris put everything on hold and went into the hospital directly. He lay on his back on the rolling bed and looked at the ceiling. As the nurse interrogated him as to his most recent bowel movements and his drinking habits, he mocked her primitive pencil and paper. She ought to have an electronic notebook! Was this a hospital or a museum? Actually what he was thinking was how fond he was of this old town, this old life. Perhaps he would die on the table. When the nurse went away he allowed himself a few nostalgic tears.

Mo, or Mao, was a futurist. He wrote a syndicated newspaper column under the name Dr. Destiny and gave seminars to businessmen on the benefits to be had from the electronic highway, camera telephones, and virtual sex. He had started out life as a teacher, had gone through graduate studies in education when that was invented, then sociology when that was invented, and now he just had a habit of sussing out what came next. It was easy to be an expert on the future because most people were so tied up in the past. Not Mao! He embraced the information explosion, audiotext, the interactive television screen as if he had been waiting for them his whole life.

We have to keep company with the new, he was certain of that, and with this certainty he became a leader of those thousands, tens of thousands, perhaps hundreds of thousands, who read his columns. He was convinced no one needed technical genius. What people needed to know was how to adapt. For this reason, the column tended toward advice. He got letters: Dear Dr. Destiny, my daughter-in-law wants to communicate with me by e-mail, she says the telephone is an intrusion, what should I do? Dear Dr. Destiny, my dictionary on CD-ROM won't decrunch, what do you recommend? Dear Dr. Destiny, my husband keeps killing women in his Fictional World CD-ROM Adventure Series, should I worry?

He wanted a local anesthetic so he could watch, but they wouldn't go that far. He was saying that he found that archaic and antidemocratic when the anesthetist came up. He counted up to twelve and was out. Only a few weeks later, he was back in the office, looking so well. Mao, Mao, the well-wishers chimed, pumping his arm, youngsters of thirty-five they were.

Morris himself was stunned. It wasn't just the pinkness of his face, the general good circulation that made his spine tingle after morning stretches. It wasn't only the spring in his step. He felt younger. He felt yearnings that were so unfamiliar he questioned his doctors about the medication. It was only something to suppress his body's immune system so he wouldn't reject the new heart, he was assured.

The very mention of rejection made him babble, "Oh, don't misunderstand me," he said. He certainly wouldn't have rejected the new heart. But there was a process. He had to get used to it, didn't he? That's what Flo said. He had taken to meeting Flo in a cafe for coffee in the mornings before going in to work.

"It races," he complained to Flo. She was drinking decaf, but he had found he could go back to a cappuccino, no problem.

"Maybe it's all that caffeine you're taking in," said Flo.

"Not that kind of racing," said Morris. "It's other things set it going." He pressed his lips together somewhat prissily and directed his clear eyes out the window to the street. It was December now but there was no snow. The lampposts in this part of town had been festooned with thick ropes of false pine, plastic silver bells, and red ribbon. In the pale morning light they looked anemic.

"Oh, do tell," said Flo. She was quick to laugh, quick to cry, a softhearted woman and a good manager. She loved her uncle, and she would inherit his company.

"Dumb things, like—" twenty-year-old androgynes in jeans with a rip across the thigh, he thought. He couldn't tell her that. "Things I haven't thought about for years," he said. "The full moon last night. Dreadful music by groups with names like Tragically Hip. Sylvester Stallone movies."

"Your heart is young," she grinned.

"Yes," said Mo. "Precisely."

A brief jealous pang crossed Flo's face. He had decades on her. She had got used to patronizing him. Now the tables had been turned. Suppose he outlived her?

"My heart is young. That means more than just a fresh muscle," he said. "Have you ever heard of organ memory?"

Florence adopted the skeptical expression that she always wore when Mo dilated on the future. But it was difficult; sooner or later people would be taking whatever he said seriously.

"No," said Florence. "Don't tell me."

"Physicians understand that the brain is just one part of the body, one more organ. There's nothing select or exclusive about it. But we assume that only the brain has memories. Wrong!" He was perched on the edge of his chair wagging his index finger. He was able to bend it at the first knuckle, so that, as he shook it before your eyes, the finger gave the fleeting, bizarre impression of an arrow broken at the tip.

"Your entire body has memories. You know how a dog that has been beaten flinches when you raise your hand? This is not a brain signal, it happens too quickly for that. The poor cur's spine, his ears, his forelegs remember being beaten and that is why, when a hand is raised, he goes into protective position."

"Indeed," said Florence. "Do tell, Dr. Destiny."

"You see, so organs have memories! Kidneys have memories. A liver has a memory. A stomach anticipates a good meal. Genital organs have memories, of course!"

Florence went dead silent.

Mo's lips moved and settled, moved and settled again as he thought.

"They may have memories," remarked Florence at last. "But they have no conscience."

Mo placed his crooked finger on his chin playfully.

"Is that a sexist comment?"

"Why should it be?" said Florence. "I made no distinctions, male or female. In fact, if I were to think about it, I'd say women have less guilt in that regard than men."

"You surprise me, dear," said Mo.

"You used to be old, and now you're young again. You've forgotten about the middle years."

"Anyway, anyway," Mo went on. "It follows, of course. What I say now will be of no surprise to you. The heart has its memories."

She nodded. "It has that reputation already."

"My heart has its memories. My new heart. The difficulty is, they aren't my memories! My heart, the heart that is beating in me now, has been taken from the body where it lived, but it has not left everything behind. In its very beat is the imprimatur of a seventeen-year-old girl."

"And the heart that you had removed? Where are its memories?" asked Florence.

"Not altogether lost. I still have my own brain, my own lungs, my own thyroid. But something new has been added. I notice so many changes in myself."

Florence gathered her purse and the check, and stood up to leave. "It's all grist for the mill, isn't it? The body of the future, with its upgraded mechanism. It's wonderful, Mo, that this should happen to you and no one else."

He followed behind, talking doggedly and wagging the confusing forefinger. "It's a question of what I feel. I feel so strange. It's as if I'm receiving messages in a language I have forgotten."

One of Mo's friends died; he went to the funeral. It was something he did often. This time he enjoyed it a great deal. He enjoyed all the crying and the fond laughter, couldn't help smiling and giggling as one after another, the old folk who were his contemporaries shuffled up to shake hands with the bereaved. Their weighted jowls he found particularly hilarious.

"My you look well," they said disapprovingly.

Mo had thrown himself into the arms of a man he knew only slightly and liked not a bit, and was sobbing on his shoulder.

"I am well," he howled. "I just haven't got control over my emotions."

When he stopped crying he began to giggle. "I'm sorry, I'm so sorry," said Mo. "It just doesn't seem real to me, that George is gone."

They nodded understanding—Mo was not really himself, it was only to be expected, after major surgery too.

Being Jewish, Mo didn't celebrate Christmas. He found it grossly sentimental, and he was frequently churlish in the holiday season. But this year was different. He was touched by the mechanical toys in Eatons' windows; the pealing of church bells gave him chills; he was shaken to the point of tears when carolers in the shopping mall blocked his exit and sang "Good King Wenceslas" with giant smiles and well-articulated lips. Released, he went away humming. "Heat was in the very sod, that the saint had printed."

Mo had other new feelings. He wanted to get out, to get away. He took to walking, exploring himself and the city. There was snow, this Christmas. He went into a shoe store on Queen Street and came out wearing Dr. Martens. They were wonderful boots, he discovered; he liked the squeak they made on the dry snow behind him.

His Dr. Martens led him to places he didn't know. The Copa, where Bare Naked Ladies were playing. He who had never stood in line waited three hours for the doors to open at midnight. With a toque pulled down over his ears and his vigorous circulation he didn't look so very old, he thought. The girls with shaved heads and white falls of straight hair over their raccoon-like eyes looked at him once and looked away. It was not friendly but it was not rejection either, and he was grateful. He took out his electronic notebook and doodled a bit, sent himself some faxes home so there would be something there to greet him. He could call this research. His heart thumped on, happy, and the messages of sadness that he had been receiving, which were too heavy for him to bear, stopped coming.

But when he came home the faxes, popping up on his screen after he dialed in, were of no comfort. When he lay down at last to sleep, at three o'clock in the morning, the heart did not want to sleep. It beat on, quickly, urgently.

"Get out of bed! There's no time," said his heart. "The sky is black, shining and clean. At night everything looks brand new."

Though he was tired, he got out of bed and dressed for walking. "You'll be the death of me," he grumbled. "It's not only the ticker you know, it's the back and the legs."

His heart had no mercy. "Outside of Toronto you can see the stars better," it whispered.

And so you could.

He drove to the Kortright Conservation Area. The road was covered with snow. The trees were towering, laden with white, mysteriously creaking under their burden. There was a barrier across the road. Mo parked the car and slid under the bar. His Dr. Martens squeaked on the dry snow. There was not a mark on it anywhere, only his footsteps.

"Heat was in the very sod," he sang under his breath. "There's no worry about us getting lost, is there? Police or anybody can just follow my steps."

It had been hard to learn to talk to his heart, it being a girl's and all. He had adopted this fond, indulgent tone.

His heart skipped gaily.

"Don't do that," he complained, "You scare me."

It calmed down. Together they walked down the road.

"My boyfriend used to bring me here in his dad's pickup," his heart confided. It spoke to him softly, with a lisp, or a flutter, probably something to do with that valve that didn't close too well. He loved the voice of his heart. "There's a place up here where we used to park."

He walked along the curve of the road. He could see taillights in there. A black Dodge pickup. There was a painful beating in his chest.

"Don't look," he said. "What color was his truck?"

"Black," she said.

"This one is red."

"I can tell when you lie. You're just trying to protect me," said his heart. He felt a wringing sensation in his chest. "It's him, isn't it? He never loved me!" his heart sobbed.

"There there, there there," he said. "Don't let it get to you," he said. "He's just a kid, you know what I mean? He's gotta live, doesn't he? He's probably on someone's shoulder about you. What was his name?"

"Brian," whispered his heart brokenly.

Mao felt a keen intellectual rage at Brian's callousness, sharpened by his heart's soft weeping.

"We've got to work together here," he said. "Listen to me, I am older and smarter."

"That's what you think," it sniffed. "But you'd be nothing without me."

"How right you are!" he laughed. He realized it was not wise to think of himself as above his heart. He'd been getting away with it all his life. He guessed that the old heart—where was it now?—had more or less given up on him.

They followed their own footsteps slowly back in the snow, Mo and his soft new heart, and drove home. Mo wasn't worried about rejecting his heart anymore. He was worried about his heart rejecting him. "You're an old fart, aren't you?" he imagined it saying. "I used to drive a newer model."

Mo cried himself to sleep. It was a luxury he'd never before allowed himself. The next morning his eyes were clear and he felt wonderful.

On Christmas Eve Mao went out with some of the young people from his office. They stood in a circle on street corners in Cabbagetown, singing carols. His new favorite was "The Holly and the Ivy."

"Let's do 'The Holly' again," he kept saying, until they all laughed at him. But when everyone kissed good-bye to go home to bed, his heart began to hurt again. "Don't leave me alone," it cried, especially when the young men turned away with their arms around the women.

"You are a sensitive thing, aren't you?" he said. The heart didn't answer.

"You wouldn't want me to get in trouble," he scolded. But his heart wasn't speaking to him.

"All right," he said, "all right." He tried the only way he knew to pacify it. He got in his car and drove up to the conservation area.

The pine trees stood heavily in their snow draperies. Again it was a still clear night, perfect for viewing Santa Claus and his reindeer ride across the sky.

"You don't still believe, do you?" he teased his heart. "They didn't give me a four year old by mistake?"

He tried to make the turn into the conservation area, but the heart started to protest. He eased back onto the highway and kept on going north to 88. "This one?" he asked.

His heart was humming now.

It was a century village. The houses were wide solid Victorians made of red Ontario brick. Highway 88 went right through on Main Street, past the Brewer's Retail, the Home Hardware, the antique stores. There was a dark patch, the park, where a shadowy gazebo squatted under bare oaks. The church was dark stone, with a trio of spires that sailed upward into the darkness.

"This doesn't look right," said Mao. "You've done something to this town. That's a very old church. Where did it come from?"

"School trip. Northern France," said his heart. "I fell for the gothic arches and the gargoyles."

The cathedral was a great construct, a medieval bishop's wet dream set down there between Lake Huron and Toronto. Mao had never been one for old churches. But that was before. Now, the delicate reaching spires made his heart sing; the heavy cavernous base with its vaulted arches, its open doorway, was like the earth itself. It had belfries and buttresses and pinnacles galore; it was a froth of stone, all glowing gold from a light somewhere. Mo sat at the wheel of his car, contemplating. His heart had stilled. And he was at a loss for a theory.

People might mistake this for a religious moment, he thought. It is not one. It may be spiritual, it may be aesthetic, it may even be hallucinatory. Certainly it is a celebration. This cathedral is a manifestation, a visitation, a virtual something or other . . . I cannot name it.

Finally, he pulled around to the parking lot behind. There was another car there. He parked and walked into the little field of gravestones.

"I guess we had to do this," said his heart. "Hope you don't mind."

Toward the back there was a cluster of wreaths on the ground. It was the newest set of graves. Of course, he thought, this was the first Christmas without their children for four sets of parents. There was someone sitting on the ground, her back leaning against a stone.

"I can't go closer," Mo said to his heart. "Someone's there."

His heart had begun to pound in a manner that made him fear for its health.

"Please, for me."

"All right, but they're going to wonder who the hell I am."

The woman was middle-aged and wrapped in a ski jacket. She wore a large neck tube pulled up to her chin. She sat quietly on a groundsheet, her head laid back against the stone, nearly asleep. It was as if she'd come for the night. She didn't look at him.

"Is it my mom?" asked his heart.

"Short brown hair, glasses?" he said.

"What is the name on the grave?"

He could just make out the fresh carving in the granite.

"Melissa Harper," he said. He was getting a very curious feeling, a sort of clammy chill around the back of his neck. "That's funny, I never said your name before."

But his heart had fallen silent now and gave him no response.

He stood there quietly for a while, before the gravestone. 1977–1993. Such a short life Melissa had had. Even her mother could have been his daughter.

Underfoot the frosted grass sparkled. When he looked up he saw the stars winking on overhead. Somewhere the old man in his sleigh was riding over the rooftops. An old man who gave things to children. They had it wrong, didn't they? It was children who gave things to old men.

"What are you doing here?" asked the brown-haired woman.

Mo's heart skipped, seemed to stop, bled a bit. He did not know what to say. They might have met, that day. It is sometimes done. The families of donors and the recipients keep in touch. Her mother had not wanted to. And there was a time factor, the rush. Mo was uncomfortable. He supposed that what he felt was slighted. Perhaps the woman thought an old Jewish man was not a fit recipient of her sweet seventeen-year-old's heart.

"It's not like you have to have me as a son-in-law or anything," he managed.

The woman snorted.

"I suppose if it weren't for me she'd be gone altogether, wouldn't she?" he tried again.

The woman stood up. Her face was gaunt, bleached of emotion, a face that, were it not for its strong bones, would have been decimated. The face of a survivor.

"I miss her so much," said her mother. "I thought I lost her once before."

"It wasn't fair," Mo agreed. He could not help but feel guilty. He stopped himself from saying that he had nothing to do with the accident.

"I know it's not your fault," said the woman, later, as they walked past the church, which was an ordinary, red brick church now, United Church, with a lit sign saying Reverend Grindstone officiated. They walked down the snowy street into town. She had cried in his arms, Melissa's mother, there beside the grave.

Once that happened, the rest was automatic. His heart, which had been exerting the strangest magnetic pull, pressed up against the wall of his chest and thanked him. He felt its need. And then it went quiet.

"It's not my fault, but I can't help but think you'd rather have someone else," said Mo. "I'm old, I'm bald, I'm paunchy . . . "

She took his arm. "I know the Chinese restaurant is open," she said. The restaurant window was decorated with gold foil wreaths: "Merry hristma" was written in a string of letters that hung in a long loop across the bottom. The restaurant was empty. A small Chinese man with spiky hair and an eerie, electric smile popped out from behind a curtain.

"Good evening, Mrs. Harper," he bowed.

"This is my friend Mao. Can we get a couple of beers?"

Mo was revising a theory. It was about duration. Organs had memories for a period of time, perhaps; they flashed powerful final signals, and then the chips died.

"You know, Mrs. Harper," he said. She hadn't told him her first name. "How long it lasts is only one aspect of a life," he said. He wagged his forefinger with its one joint bent at her. The waiter stood by. "I'll have chips and gravy, too."

Photo by Marianne Gontarz

starboys
Elissa Goldberg

Dear Anna,

I am writing this from a coffee shop. My seat is by the window. Why, you are thinking, am I sitting in a coffee shop when I have a perfectly good house to sit in? Okay, I will tell you.

Marilyn, our dear daughter, may she have a long and wonderful life, this dear child of ours who is no longer a child, decided last month to cure me. Cure me of what, I do not know. I did not ask. One day she came in. A day no different from any other, I was sitting in the living room watching the television news.

Marilyn went into the kitchen to empty her grocery bags. "Dad," she said. "I bought you new coffee. It's decaffeinated."

"What does this mean, decaffeinated?" I asked. This I said from my chair, why should I walk into the kitchen?

"Unleaded, Dad. You shouldn't be drinking regular coffee. It's a diuretic."

"Tell me, Marilyn," I said. "And what does this mean, diuretic?"

By this time she was standing in the doorway of the kitchen, folding her paper bag.

"It means it takes too much water out of you. You're too old for that."

Nu? Decaffeinated. Diuretic. Too much water. Let her do what she wants. What did I care?

I forgot about it. The next day, I got up, I fed the birds, read the newspaper, and drank my coffee. No big deal. But that afternoon, a headache. And what a headache, loud, pounding, I could not think. This was not so new to me. Headaches. They come, they go. But this one, it was different. The next day, it was still with me. And the next day also. Like a black cloud, it filled my head with thunder, everywhere I went.

When Marilyn came on the third day, I remembered. "Marilyn," I said, "this decaffeinated coffee, however you call it, it is killing me."

"Ha, ha," she laughed. "It's not killing you, Dad. It's good for you."

"It is murdering me. Go, buy me some coffee. Or tomorrow you will be pouring this decaffeinated coffee on my grave."

"Dad," she said. "You have a headache? You'll get over it. It's not the decaf that's giving it to you. It's from no caffeine. It'll stop soon." She laughed again, and then she was gone. This is what she does. Comes into my house, checks things off her list, and then disappears.

I sat down. "Okay," I said to the floor. "I will buy my own coffee."

It was a cold day. No rain, clear sky, but a wind that shook the trees against the houses. I walked to the Fred Meyers grocery store. But before I got there, a few blocks away, I saw Joel Weinstein. Dr. Weinstein. Flash, we used to call him, do you remember, for the way he was always dressed. Always the most dapper fellow, black hat, grey coat, wing tips when we were still wearing loafers. A snappy dresser.

He was getting out of his car. How did I recognize him? I don't know. I had not seen him in years. He moved in different circles than ours after a while. We were not, you remember, as well-to-do as he. Still, I knew it was him.

"Flash," I said, "Dr. Weinstein." And I held out my hand.

He looked at my hand. Then he stared into my face with his runny grey eyes.

"Jack Manasky," I said.

"Yes," he said. "Of course." And then, Anna, he began to cry. Water dripped through the creases by his eyes, and his breath broke like teacups from his mouth. I looked down, I should not see another man cry.

"I'm sorry. Excuse me," he said. He did not have a handkerchief. And I did not offer him mine.

"You want to talk?" I asked.

He shook his head. "It's life." Then he told me that he lost his Rebecca four months earlier. A stroke, one leg and one arm useless, her speech hitting a wall in her head before ever reaching her lips. A prisoner in her own body until the blood in her brain broke another time, with mercy.

"I am a dead man," he said, his arms stretched out. Spittle dropped from his chin.

"Do you have time now?" I said. "You want to have a bite to eat, a cup of coffee?"

"No," he said. "Another time." He shook my hand, and then walked away. Not even a hat on his head.

I watched him walk, Anna. A lost man. His coat stained. His figure bent like the head of a cane.

I turned to go on my way, when what did I see? A coffee store. A store selling nothing but coffee, they have such things these days. Nu, Dr. Joel Weinstein, he saved my life.

I went inside this store. Starbins, it is called. Or Starboys.

"I want a cup of coffee," I said to the young man.

"Short or tall," he said.

"I am short," I said, and he laughed. He told me his name was Tim.

"Tim, I am Jack," I said. "Give me a cup of coffee. " And in a minute, Anna, magic. My headache was gone.

Nu, so the next day, I did the same thing. And the next day, again. By now it is my routine. Wake up, feed the birds, read up on Mr. President Clinton's new ideas. Then I walk to Starbuds, buy myself a nice cup of coffee from Tim.

"Tim," I say. "You don't know, but you and Dr. Weinstein saved my life."

Still, this whole time, Anna, I was thinking about him, Flash. I remember that pain. It is like a dagger, every time you take a breath. Sometimes even now, six years after you have left me, may you rest in peace, I feel it. The memories, they choke me.

I remember your last two weeks in the hospital. I walked like a machine. I would sit you up in bed, your skin white like the moon. Four pillows it took, do you remember? Two behind your back, and one on either side so your thin body could be straight. And then you let me comb your hair. Such thin hair that you would not let them cut. You watched the trees out your window. Sometimes our eyes met. We had no words.

When you died, I sat by your bed for a long time. No one came, not a nurse, nobody from the family. Maybe they all thought things were fine, seeing me in that chair. They did not know I could not move. I didn't know that I could.

Remembering these things, I thought, who better than myself to talk to Dr. Weinstein? Someone else who has gone through what he is going through. So I called him up on the telephone. I said, "Dr. Weinstein, this is Jack Manasky."

He is a bit deaf, this man. "Who?" he said.

"Jack Manasky. I saw you the other day," I said.

"Frank?" he said.

I was ready to hang up. But he caught on. As soon as he knew who I was, he was silent.

I asked him, "Listen, you want to meet me for lunch? Maybe we could meet at the Jewish Center?"

He was still silent. So I repeated myself. I should have known to say every-thing twice.

"No," he said. His voice, Anna, was like a buzz saw.

"No?" I said. "You do not want to?"

"I will not go out with you," he said, and then he hung up the phone. What could I do? It is not often that I feel like a teenager, but I felt like one then. He does not like me, I thought. He has never liked me. We were never really friends. Maybe his family has taken up all his time. He is too busy.

Then I told myself other things. Who needs him? Like a hole in my head, I need him. I, too, am busy. I was not even thinking of him for twenty years before I saw him that day.

Still, I tried again. One night I could not sleep. At about two o'clock in the morning, I had an idea to call Flash Weinstein to invite him to the movies. Perfect, I thought. He doesn't want to talk, he won't have to talk. We'll be two old friendly faces watching a screen together. But I was smart. I waited until eight o'clock to call him.

"Hello, Flash," I said. "This is Jack Manasky. You want to see a movie with me?"

"Do I want to be a what?" he said.

"A movie. A movie. You want to go see a movie with me?"

"*Oi, got,*" he said, and I could tell he was crying. Eight o'clock in the morning and this man was crying. "No," he said. "Let me call you."

I put down the telephone and stared at it. Then I walked slowly to buy my cup of coffee.

That morning, Marilyn came over.

"Dad," she said. "You are not drinking coffee at all anymore? You can drink this stuff. This stuff isn't bad for you."

"Marilyn, it's bad for me."

"Dad," she said. Her face looked torn, crumpled like a piece of paper. "Dad, I got you this. It's special coffee. It's not bad for you like that other stuff you were drinking."

"Marilyn," I said. "I like my coffee. When I want you to buy me different coffee I will let you know."

Marilyn didn't look at me after that. She reached for her purse. "Okay," she said, but I saw her hand shake. And, as she walked to her car, twice she blew her nose.

I sat down in my chair. I felt heavy as an elephant. Sometimes, Anna, since you have gone, I do not know what to do.

Until we meet again,

Jack

senior golfer
Marilyn Stacy

The up side is
he's finally shooting his age.

The down side is
he has to keep finding new partners.

His wife says
look for younger friends.
Maybe they'll last longer.

Photo by Lori Burkhalter-Lackey

forgive us our trespasses
Rose Hamilton-Gottlieb

"Note the gender-free color. No wimpy pink for this girl," Ted says. Evie watches doubtfully as her son-in-law turns down a corner of the yellow receiving blanket, places his firstborn's shoulders even with the fold, and tucks and winds it around the wiggling baby until even her hands are imprisoned. "It's sort of like making a burrito," he jokes. He nestles her on his shoulder.

"I thought swaddling went out with the Middle Ages."

"The nurse said it makes her feel safe. Daddy will always keep his princess safe," he croons in baby-talk tones. "Okay, Baby Burrito, in the oven you go."

Evie winces, reminds herself Lori is too young to be frightened by the image. Ted will have to learn to watch what he says.

He lays her in the cradle. "So she can see the bright colors." He nods toward a Jasper Johns print on the wall nearby. "Can't start developing her taste in art too soon."

Evie represses a dry comment that she'll hide the Norman Rockwell in her own living room when they come to visit. She doesn't tell him her granddaughter can't see any further than the bumper pad lining the cradle. As she leans over to smooth the blanket, Lori's blue eyes—were ever a newborn's eyes so bright?—momentarily focus and lock onto hers. She's struck by the wonder of . . . what? Another chance for the human race to get it right? If only Glen could hold his granddaughter. She forces back capricious widow tears.

Ted sniffs. "You smell pretty, but did you invest in Elizabeth Arden?"

Only mildly insulted, she manages a light laugh. "I read somewhere a baby remembers with her nose. This is my visiting Grandma fragrance." She turns to go. "I'll be at the clothesline, then down by the willow practicing tai chi." She took up tai chi chuan last year, at the suggestion of a grief counselor. It's an easy form of tai chi, developed for the American short attention span, the teacher joked. A fad, she thought then, but it was one empty evening filled.

Now, when anger at her loss and fears about the future close in, it's as if the movements open dark corners of her mind to light and air. And release.

She senses as much as hears Ted's sudden intake of breath and looks back at him. There's something in his face that wasn't there a moment ago.

"I'd rather you didn't do that in the yard," he says.

Maybe he's teasing again. "Why not?"

"Because the neighbors might see you."

She laughs. "I expect they'll get over it."

"I don't like it either." His voice is flat.

"You'll get over it too," she counters, before the tone of his voice registers. She looks at him. His fair skin, prone to sunburn and allergic rashes, is mottled with anger. She feels the usual sickening paralysis at the first suggestion of confrontation, like thick sap in her legs.

"You're serious!"

"Yes, I'm serious. Rita wouldn't like it either."

"How do you know she wouldn't?"

"She's my wife."

She starts to say, "And I'm her mother," but chokes off the retort.

Shaken, she turns and flees with a basket of laundry to the clothesline. Hands trembling, she drapes three wet diapers over her left arm and scoops up four clothespins with her right hand, a technique learned thirty years ago. She pins the diapers to the clothesline, lifting her arms without a twinge of arthritis. When she first took up tai chi, she could hardly bend her knees for the back-and-forth leg movements, and her arms ached in the "Cosmic Consciousness" pose. Her balance hadn't been so good either.

She has looked forward to this, even brought a dozen diapers with her, guessing correctly that Rita wouldn't know disposable diapers are useless as burp cloths. She bends and lifts and pins one corner to another, in a rhythm that connects her to past generations, a rhythm broken by the new mother's best friend, the automatic dryer. That—and the spring morning—mock her. So does the willow tree that has beckoned since her arrival last week.

She hangs the last diaper. A breeze lifts and fills them. Like sails. No, flags. Flags to celebrate birth. Flags of surrender. No, she won't surrender so easily. This is his home, but she'll at least have her say.

Ignoring the censor in the back of her mind that says, *Wait, time out, think,* she stomps into the kitchen. He's loading the dishwasher. She gets a glass and runs water from the tap. What she plans is to hit and run. "I guess it's a good thing you settled in this community," she says. "Some of your provincial ideas fit in well here."

"Just what do you mean by that?"

"Just what I said. In San Francisco people practice tai chi in parks. And in broad daylight." She dips each word in sarcasm.

He shoves the dishwasher door shut. The glasses inside clatter. "Do you know how that sounds?"

She wavers. Yes, she knows. But she won't call the words back. She ignores the warning voice, *This is not why you came all this way,* and pushes the point. "You act as if there's something wrong with it. Why in China—"

"That's China. This is Oregon. I have to live with these people."

She wants to point out the contempt inherent in "these people," but this has gone far enough. She casts about for a way to end it.

He speaks first. "What if I brought a nudist friend to your house, and he walked around naked in your backyard? How would you like that?"

Fear overtakes her. This is no hit and run. It's as if she's trapped at the scene of an accident and a policeman just pulled up. It occurs to her that if Glen were here, no, if Glen were even alive, Ted would show more respect. She goes weak with a familiar wave of hopelessness, and on its heels, defeat and resignation. "Look, the baby kept us both up last night. We're tired."

"Speak for yourself." She cringes at the contempt in his voice.

"All right. I'm exhausted. I'll be in my room."

She walks blindly down the hall to the guest room and closes the door behind her. Her stomach churns, not only with anger, but with embarrassment. She didn't come here to be a problem; she came to help. To be useful. She's grateful Rita is out shopping. Maybe she will stay away long enough for her to practice tai chi. Long enough for the tai chi to dissolve her anger.

She opens the window onto a front yard that is still dirt. Across the street a bulldozer flattens the land for another house. Beyond that is the orchard of the original farm. Maybe she could trespass and find a nice spot under an apple tree. But no, the neighbors might think she's . . . what? A hippie?

A breeze blows the lace curtains aside. It carries the scent of apple blossoms, but the bulldozer is too loud, so she closes the sash. She kicks off her shoes and shoves her open suitcase out of the way. Hands swing forward as she rocks onto her toes, then back as she moves onto her heels.

What did he mean by that nudist crack? She forces her attention to the soles of her feet. Nine rocking motions, and she completes the movement with knees bent and hands pressed down in the "Graceful Conclusion." Motionless, she stares out onto the dirt. It's stuffy in here. She thinks of violets beneath the willow at the water's edge. She closes her eyes, breathes into the t'an tien.

After all, it's his house. She remembers what it was like to grow up in a farm community where eyes keep watch for differences. But how dare he?

Right knee bent, she sinks onto that foot and puts her left foot out, empty, then shifts her weight forward as she dips her arms for the "Daughter on the Mountaintop" movement. Back, forward, back. Nine times.

She hears a car. Then voices. So he's telling Rita about their little spat. He could have kept it to himself. Now Rita will play peacemaker. She sighs.

The bedroom door opens. It's Rita. Evie, who has never in her life entered a bedroom without first knocking, and who thought she had taught her daughter this simple courtesy, swallows her irritation. New mothers get special dispensation for rude behavior. She swallows, too, her widow's fear that she's no longer considered worthy of even the consideration of a knock on the door. Deliberately ignoring the intrusion, she lifts her arms for the "Daughter in the Valley" movement.

Oblivious to the obvious body language, Rita comes close and says, "It's not just Ted, Mom. I don't like it either."

Pausing in the "Graceful Conclusion," she looks at Rita. Thin with a smattering of freckles over her nose. "Little Mouse," Glen nicknamed her at birth, and it stuck until she came in from school one day in tears. She looks tired. This is causing Rita unnecessary pain. Irritation battles with anguish and wins. "I assume you don't mind if I do it in here. With the door closed."

Rita says nothing. Beats a quick retreat. Evie hears postpartum tears from without. She almost doesn't care.

She shifts from side to side, hands imitating passing clouds. Troubles are like passing clouds, she reminds herself. But now she's angry with both of them. Gradually, the air around her thickens, and she welcomes the familiar tingling in her fingers. Energy flowing. If only she could retrieve the morning.

She'd say, "I'll be in my room practicing tai chi," and he'd tease her about being a New Age old lady. She could forgive him that. But this? *Move into that space between thoughts. Think of sand spilling from one part of the body to another.* But the sand becomes angry liquid rising from the soles of her feet. Tears start. *No, empty the mind.*

For a half hour Evie moves back and forth, empty and full, yin and yang, blaming the children, blaming herself, moving in and out of that place between the beats of time where nothing matters but the joy in movement. But self-conscious about making noises foreign to this house, she dispenses with the six healing sounds. As she holds the "Cosmic Consciousness" pose, balanced on her toes with arms curved into a circle in front of her heart, she begins to sob.

She's still angry. *All right, give in to it; let it have its way.* She lies down. Stares at the ceiling. Tears bathe her face, but what does she feel? Rage, at Ted's words, at the certainty the children discussed her. But why all the tears? Tears that won't stop, she learned in grief counseling, are unshed tears from the past. She closes her eyes. *Empty the mind. Let go.* Within seconds light and color fill her vision, and into the void she inserts the question, What is it I need to look at? and waits. Colors coalesce. Images form.

She sees herself as a child, inside the Mills's Airstream travel home. Mrs. Mills squeezed in behind the built-in table, pink scalp showing in the part of her bluish hair. Mama beside her in those rimless glasses that made her small features uncompromising. Red castanets painted with yellow flowers. She takes them from Mrs. Mills's outstretched hands.

What does this have to do with Ted? *Stay with it. Stay open to buried feelings.* She leans into the memory. The Mills had stopped at the farm on their way home from Mexico. Nine-year-old Evie had followed Mama to the trailer from the front porch where she had been helping Grandma shell peas.

Real castanets! All summer she had played at being a Spanish dancer, twirling in a long skirt pinned in back to fit, snapping her fingers above her head, her teeth clamped around a cloth rose torn from a hat. She smiled a shy thank-you and turned to go, but Mrs. Mills took them back. She had only been showing them to her. Feeling stupid, Evie waited for Mama to say something, make it all right. But Mama looked embarrassed. No, ashamed. Suffocating in the small trailer, Evie scrambled to the ground.

Outside, she listened for Mama and Mrs. Mills to go on to other things so she could pretend this never happened. "Evie's so absentminded," her mother said. "Why, just the other day I came in the kitchen and she was mixing up stuff. The way kids do when you leave the house. Vinegar and mustard, whatever smelly things they can get their hands on. As I came in, she lit a match, and whatever that concoction was went *whoosh,* up in flames." Mrs. Mills clucked. "I grabbed a towel and snuffed it out. It's lucky I came in when I did or she'd have burned down the house. I have to watch her every minute."

Mama had lied about her. It was true Evie had played at mixing a magic potion and the matches were there, on the table, so naturally she had to see what would happen. And Mama had caught her. But it was she who had put out the fire, even before she knew she'd been caught.

Recognition rides in on a deep sigh. She waits for peace to descend, waits for the morning's events to shift into proper perspective, into an offense of manageable proportions. If only Glen were here. He would help her with this. She needs air. This room can no longer hold her pain. The tears have stopped, but more wait behind her eyes and in her throat. She picks up wet balls of tissues from the bed, tosses them in the wastebasket, and finds her shoes.

Outside, attracted by the smell of flowers, she takes the gravel road toward the orchard. How insulting that Ted cares more about the neighbors than he cares about her feelings. She can forgive her mother because that was a long time ago, and because, as a mother herself, she has made her own mistakes. But she'll have to practice a lot more tai chi before she can forgive him. She'll go home. Tomorrow, if possible. If she leaves before the baby gets her days and nights straightened out, he'll wish he'd treated her better. But there's no relief in her decision. Only tears. Irritating tears of self-pity. Had she not gone through the change years ago, she'd blame it on hormones.

She feels exposed on the road, so in spite of the No Trespassing sign, she climbs a fence and takes a path into the neglected orchard. Somebody will just have to forgive her this trespass.

She goes in among the blossoming trees. Apple trees older than she with thick, gnarled trunks. No doubt they'll be cut down to make way for more houses, ruining the area's provincial charm. Overhead, white clouds stack up against a brilliant blue sky. An unexpected gift. The promise of peace.

She turns back, through the avenue of apple blossoms. She stops on the gravel road to pick a dandelion. Stalling. She dreads the call to the airlines, feels a pang at the thought of leaving the child. As she turns into the front yard, Ted comes out, carrying Lori, still wrapped in the gender-free yellow receiving blanket. In his big arms, the yellow blanket looks touchingly brave. He takes long strides across the dirt yard. She squares her shoulders. She'll tell him she's leaving before he can ask her to go.

But he speaks first. "We have to talk. I haven't been able to think of anything else since this morning."

She waits. All right, if he wants to talk. How much should she share with him? Can she make him understand insights she only half understands herself?

"You know very well why we're here in this backwater. I'm in environmental cleanup, remember? My company sends me where the toxic dumps are. I belong in the city. We go there every chance we get . . . "

What on earth is he talking about?

He holds Lori on one arm and gestures broadly with the other. "We go to plays. I subscribe to the *Wall Street Journal.* Our house is full of Jasper Johns and Paul Klee and David Hockney. How dare you call me provincial?"

Why, she shamed him too. It's as if she sees him for the first time. Sees him as a little boy not quite good enough in someone else's eyes. She hurt his feelings. The idea brings her up short. He found something she said important enough to be wounded by it. She suddenly likes him better.

He goes on to list his liberal political credentials, but she barely listens, struck as she is by Lori, who stares at her father's face as if hanging on every word. Evie wants to interrupt him, say to him, Yes, I shamed you and you shamed me. And how soon will it be before one of us shames this child? For we will, you know, in an offhand remark or in some unrealized neglect or some careless gratification of our own egos. Or will it be through fear of what the neighbors will think?

He stops talking, as if he has run down and is waiting for some response from her. She meets his gaze, full of . . . what? Anger, certainly, but underneath is a plea for validation. *And from her.*

"Why, Ted," she says, surprised how easy it is. "I didn't mean you were provincial. I only meant you had some provincial ideas. In that department,

I'm sure I out-provincial you." Having forgiven him, she's confident in his forgiveness.

"Well, all right," he says. How dark the circles are under his eyes.

"Where's Rita?"

"Napping. She's pretty upset." His tone is accusing.

Yes, she would be. Evie reaches for the baby, the only way she knows to atone for her self-preoccupation. "You rest too. That's why I'm here." She laughs. "Perhaps we all have a mild case of postpartum depression." He gives her the baby. A smile tugs at his mouth.

Lori wiggles in the blanket, but Evie resists the urge to loosen it. She will not be one of those grandmothers who does everything the opposite of what the parents want. Anyway, Lori will survive the physical swaddling. But in what other ways will her parents, enlightened as they are, swaddle her? For they will. No matter how much they love her, no matter how often they use phrases like child development and self-esteem. They will do it because of their own wounds. Or out of the press of daily living and the daily frustrations of raising a child. They will do it as surely as if their job is to inflict a wound. An image pops into her mind: Rita at five, sobbing over the suddenly hated nickname, "Little Mouse."

As she turns, a cloud passes over the sun, obscuring it so that light pours from around it, turning the cloud bank salmon against the azure sky. A tai chi sky. As if riding on a beam of light, with clarity that comes when time stops, the rest of that long-ago memory rises to consciousness.

When she left the shadow of the trailer, she sought out Grandma, still on the porch shelling peas. She smiled her Grandma smile that said Evie could do no wrong. Glad for the excuse to lean into her soft body, Evie sat beside her and reached across her lap for a handful of green pods.

Now, Evie closes her eyes and imagines she hears peas bounce off the sides of the enamel pan, smells the Palmolive soap Grandma washed with every morning, hears her answer to all hurts, "There, there, fifty years from now this won't seem like anything." Remembering this now, the last of her pain falls away like those peas falling. She will stay out her visit. She must come as often as she can, wearing her Grandma fragrance and her Grandma smile that will tell Lori she can do no wrong.

to my granddaughter's
future lover

Ellen Kort

Late some winter night   years from now
you may be the one to touch her cheek
her arm   the soft geometry where her body
ends and your hand begins   There may be
a low moon   snow   a murmur of owl
You may find comfort in the way her arm

covers your heart   the weight of your leg
over hers   Your breath may be warm
Your dreams may wander like stars
hurrying home   You may not know
that the future is something less
than a shrug of cells   the body's river

twisting through old tangled roots
that our worst losses are not in the past
but those directly ahead   You may not
yet know how kinship digs deeper
than any spring or cellar
is older than the green curve of seed fern

or the brightness in eyes   Yesterday
I made a drum   chiseled and sanded
the sounding edge   cut and soaked
goat skin   lacing it from top
to bottom   coming up from underneath
pulling it tight without tearing

When it dried and I thumbed it
for the first time   it was the same beat
her heart made when I held her
soon after she was born   how she nestled
against me   into my breast pouch
of warmth and sound

that timeless moment when what we gain
becomes equal to what we lose
and we enter   breathless
and unafraid   into our own perfect life

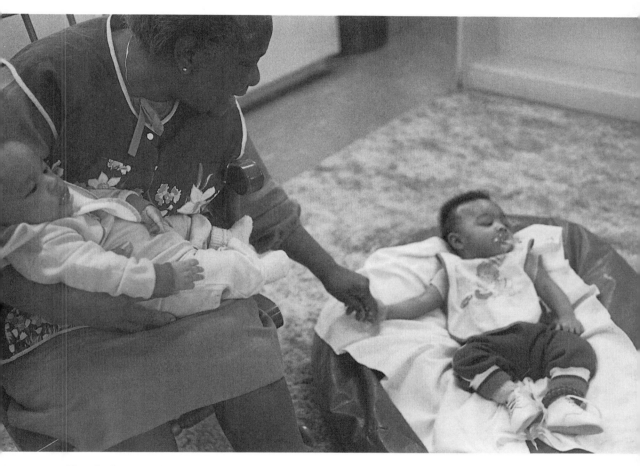

Photo by Marianne Gontarz

155

figure of speech
Nancy Means Wright

Around a curve on a brushy
trail I come on a pair

of trees: one behind
the other like dancers

on a bar. Their trunks
crane forward,

leaves sweep the ground
like a girl

throwing her hair
over her head to dry,

or the coupled buds
of a sapling

straining for accents
of April.

When Zoë springs
up laughing

and runs back
to meet my unsure foot-

fall I don't know if I'm
about to embrace

a tree or a grand-
daughter. In any case

I'm transported.

Photo by Marilyn Nolt

wishing for maybes
Nancy Moser

*"Hear your father's instruction, and do not forsake your mother's teaching;
Indeed, they are a graceful wreath to your head and ornaments about your
neck."* —Proverbs 1: 8–9

The Grandparents

On bad days, I wish I'd never answered the phone that Tuesday night.

It was a fluke we were home in the first place. Manny was in the car, within
seconds of tooting the horn at me, while I rummaged through my desk looking
for the tickets to the travelogue we were late for. *If only I hadn't forgotten the
tickets; if only I'd cleaned my desk the week before; if only . . .*

It solved nothing to think of the *if onlys*. I was in the house, the phone rang, I
answered it. And our lives were changed.

I grabbed the phone and shoved it in the crook of my neck, my hands still digging through the piles on my desk.

"Mom, Jake's left! He's gone. Sarah's crying, Jon threw up, and the soup boiled
over. I can't deal with it, Mom. Can I bring the kids over? Please?"

I stopped looking for the tickets. I heard Manny toot the horn. We wouldn't be
late for the travelogue. We weren't going.

"Bring them over," I said.

That was nine months ago.

To be perfectly honest—a trait that is more and more dear to me—if we had
missed that particular phone call, there would've been another. Life-changing
phone calls are persistent and inevitable.

On good days I look at our grandchildren, Sarah and Jonathan, and smile at the fine job they're doing coloring their pictures or setting the table. And when they climb into my lap at night and nuzzle their downy cheeks against mine, I praise God for the love He brought into our lives.

This dizzying combination of regret and gratitude is natural now. The tranquillity of our retirement years has been replaced by the chaos and tedium of raising two small children. Loud voices. Rigid schedules.

It's harder on Manny. Even though I'd long ago left behind thoughts of homework and skinned knees, I was infinitely more prepared to take on the responsibility of our grandchildren than he was. He'd never witnessed the day-to-day dealings of broken shoelaces and sack lunches with our own daughter. He'd been at work. But work was over for him. He paid his dues, and his lofty dreams of retirement—our lofty dreams—were cut short as we backtracked twenty years to the sights and sounds of parenthood.

He is the one who voices the question we both want answered. He is the one who lets his indignation show. When I see his lips pull tight and the crease between his brows deepen, I shuffle the children away to another room, to some other point of interest, so I can return and hear his resentment alone. The children have heard too many arguments in their short lives. I try to spare them one more.

"Life isn't fair," I remind him.

His head drifts back and forth like a pendulum.

"We can't blame Sheila," I say. "She's had a hard time. Jake leaving her with no job and two small children. It was too much."

"It was too easy," he says. "We made it too easy for her to give up." His voice rises above the television. I check the hall to make sure the children are tucked away. He goes on. "Sheila calls. Her voice grabs us around the neck. She begs us to take the kids. What do we do? We take them. What does she do? She gets a smaller apartment and the chance to live the single life she missed by getting pregnant in high school. She's happy."

He makes it sound like a sin. Maybe it is: finding happiness at the expense of others.

I nod, agreeing with him, but not egging him on. I've heard it before. I've felt it before. Six months ago I would've argued with him—a defender of the familial roots. But after having had the children so long, my defenses are shallow; my guilt is deep. I pray about that. About a lot of things.

The children are no longer visitors. Their Barbie dolls and race cars are at home on the shelves in the family room, right next to my needlepoint and Manny's fishing magazines. There is an odd comfort in the sounds of their footfalls. Their laughter weaves its way through the rungs of the chairs and echoes in the cookie jar. They belong here. They are ours.

But I feel cheated. I glance at the pile of travel brochures teasing from the pocket of the recliner. Hawaii, Alaska, England. Will these places remain exotic? Will they ever become a part of our conversation and our memories? *"This reminds me of the sunset we saw on Maui." "Those birds remind me of the ravens at the Tower of London."*

Sometimes I want to grab Sheila by the arms and shake her. Make her take back the responsibility that is hers. Make her take back the duties of motherhood.

And let us be grandparents again.

The Mother

I'm so tired I'm afraid I'll never wake up. It's not a body tired, it's a brain tired. If only I had a switch to turn off the clutter racing through my mind.

I stare at the TV, letting the drivel fill my head with fake laughter and whiny jingles. Odd how it helps. I take off my earrings and cover my feet with the afghan, ready to fall asleep on the couch. I go to sleep to the babble of TV and I wake to it. It is my consolation prize for an empty bed.

Not that I want Jake back. It's better he's gone. I just wish *I* had been the one to leave. Let him handle the problems left behind. Let me be the one to find a new life somewhere else.

I haven't heard from him. You'd think he could at least send me a few dollars and the kids a card on their birthdays. Something. He may be dead. It bothers me that I don't care, that I only want to know so I can go on with my life. Put it behind me.

I know my parents think I'm sleeping around in my "single's pad." They have their reasons. I did get pregnant my senior year and I did marry Jake, so I guess they're justified in doubting my morals, if not my common sense.

But I'm not sleeping around. I could. But I'm not. I've changed. My life has changed me. I've gone out twice in the last nine months. Once to a movie I slept through and once to dinner where I was supposed to be the dessert. I find the idea of getting involved with a man unnerving. I don't want to be *needing,* but it makes it hard when needing and wishing are intertwined like the strands of a rope.

Truth is, I've come to realize my parents are right. Were always right. I sold myself cheap for a few moments of fun. Mom wants me to start reading the Bible again. I don't like everything it says, but I'll read it for her. Maybe I need to read it. Hear it. Know it. She seems to think it's the only thing that's real.

I'm doing all right on my own. My job at the telephone company is a steady paycheck. Nice people. I get my insurance paid and holidays. It's better than Jake ever did.

But the hours are long. When I get home, the last thing I want is kids pestering, asking questions, wanting a piece of me. There aren't any pieces left.

I miss them. I miss tucking them in at night, braiding Sarah's hair and finding Jon's mini-cars under the couch and in the laundry basket. I miss the smell of them, the smell of fresh air, spilled juice, and crayons.

But I have to set such thoughts away. It's not possible. Not now. If I paid day care for Jon and for Sarah after school, I'd be bringing home piddle for a check. Besides, this apartment is barely big enough for one, much less three. And the neighborhood's not great. I wouldn't want them playing outside here.

I suppose I could've moved in with Mom and Dad. I thought of it. But this is better. Even if I don't get to see the kids every day, *they* are better. If I had moved in, there would've been arguments. My parents say I'm too lenient. Maybe so. After nine months, it's obvious their way isn't so bad. It's just not my way.

What is my way? Do I even have a way anymore?

When I see the kids, it's as if I am the grandparent. There is a wall between us that comes from being apart. I've tried to be straight with them and explain what happened between their dad and me, but who knows how much an eight and four year old understand.

Sometimes I cry. For them—and for me. I used to complain about being a stay-at-home mom. My life was wasted with two kids who didn't care what I thought and dreamed about as long as their bottoms were dry and their stomachs full. Back then I wanted a career.

Life is fickle.

I wish I had a future to think about. I wish I had their future to think about.

I wish I could be a mom again.

The Children

I like living with Grandpa and Grandma. Most of the time. Sometimes Grandpa huffs and puffs like he doesn't want us around, but then he flicks the tip of my nose and smiles.

My room is pink. It used to be Grandma's sewing room, but after a while she moved her sewing stuff to one side and hung pink curtains with yellow flowers. The bedspread's got stitching that makes it poofy. I've even got what Grandma calls a dresser set. She gave it to me for my birthday. It has a pink brush and comb and a mirror with a ballerina on the back. It makes me feel grown.

Jon-Jon's room is next to mine. It was the guest room. They didn't change his room 'cept to add a toy box and a shelf for his trucks and books. I like my room better even though my bed is littler than his.

Grandma makes good food, though we don't go to McDonald's or Pizza Hut as much as Mama and Daddy did. But there's always cookies. Grandma let me make the last batch by myself 'cept for the oven part. I had to yell at Jon-Jon 'cause he kept eating the dough. It wasn't my fault he fell off the chair. He stopped crying when I gave him some chocolate chips.

I wish we could watch more TV, but Grandma says we only get one hour a night 'cause she doesn't want our brains turning to mush. Grandpa and I play Go Fish and Monopoly. Jon-Jon likes to line up the plastic houses and hotels. I read a lot. Grandma helps me with the hard words. I like sitting in her lap. She smells like Ivory soap. We're reading the story of Jesus in Matthew. Jesus was a nice man. He wouldn't have left us like Daddy did.

I miss Daddy. Mama told us he left 'cause he wasn't happy but that doesn't make sense 'cause sometimes I'm not happy but I don't run away. We could've been happy. Jon-Jon and I would've helped. Mama says we're divorced now. I feel divorced. From Mama and Daddy.

I hate Mama's apartment. The walls are covered with nails for pictures—but there aren't any pictures. And the carpet smells like dog pee—but she doesn't have a dog. Every week I draw her a new picture to put on the refrigerator to try to make it nicer for her.

It's weird seeing Mama only twice a week. It takes us a while to feel normal with her, and then it's time to go home. But we do fun things. We go people watching at the mall and camp in sleeping bags on her living room floor. She lets us bring popcorn and Kool-Aid in front of the TV. Jon-Jon spilled once but she said it didn't matter, it probably made the carpet smell better.

Mama's eyes are funny, like it's hard for her to see through 'em. Sometimes she blinks real slow like they'd stay shut if she let 'em. She always acts happy in front of Grandpa and Grandma, but when we're alone her eyes change.

Last Saturday Mama took all of us out to dinner to celebrate her 'motion.

"Pretty soon we can look for a bigger apartment," she said. "One with a bedroom for you and Jon. Wouldn't that be great?"

She smiled when she said it and I smiled too. Later that night, I saw Grandpa looking at a folder showing palm trees and blue water. Maybe it'll be all right.

I've been wishing for *maybe*s a long time. Maybe it's time my *maybe*s came true.

Photo by Marianne Gontarz

the tea party
Kathie Lokken

Livvy wasn't used to being old. It still caught her by surprise when neighbors and old friends retired or moved to Florida or died. She would smile every day at the bronze baby shoes on her dresser then be startled when her children's adult voices cut over the telephone. Or when she caught sight of the children's wedding pictures on the hallway wall, hung where the baby portraits used to be.

Livvy's oldest daughter called her every day. She was local, not long-distance, and could afford to. Every evening, Livvy checked the television schedule for the name of the CBS nightly movie. Then when her daughter called at lunch and asked if she'd seen the movie the night before, Livvy could say, "Oh, you mean . . ." and supply the name. From there, her daughter would launch on a description and criticism of the movie and its actors that would last a half hour or so. Livvy could drink her tea and look out the window at her bird feeders or her neighbor's backyard and wait for her daughter's voice to stop. Then they'd say good-bye, and Livvy would breathe deeply.

Her other daughter, the youngest, was long-distance. She lived in California, which Livvy believed was as long-distance from Wisconsin as one could get. She only called once a month, and it was never the same night. Livvy found it harder to talk to this daughter. Livvy read the paper every night and made notes on the latest news developments on a pad of paper. She kept the pad by the phone in the living room, so when her California daughter called, she could share her opinion on current events. It worked most of the time, except when Livvy happened to be closer to the phone in the kitchen. Then she had to rely on her memory or her wits, which usually worked.

Livvy sighed as she looked out her kitchen window. Her neighbor Books was leaning over the fence, looking toward Livvy's house. Books's real name was Beatrice, but Livvy had called her Books since the family moved in next door thirty years ago. Besides baby things, bookshelves had been moved in. Bookshelves for every room, and Books filled them. Livvy waved at Books, through the window, and went for her sweater. The dishes needed doing, but she knew Books would wait there, by the fence, until Livvy went out. She didn't want Books to catch a cold.

Books grabbed Livvy's hands as she reached the fence. "Livvy, they're coming for me this afternoon," she whispered.

Livvy blinked and rubbed Books's hands. "Who is? For what?"

"My son and his wife. He called this morning. Said they found a nice place, a retirement community he called it, right near them. A nice bedroom, he said, and a small kitchen and my own bathroom, all in a building with other bedrooms and kitchens and bathrooms. And people to watch me, he said. He's worried, he said." Books let go of Livvy and hugged her sweater more tightly across her chest. "It's a building, Livvy, not a house. Not my house." She looked over her shoulder. "A bedroom, and a kitchen, and a bathroom."

"Didn't you know he was going to do this? Didn't he tell you?"

Books looked back. "He mentioned it, once, over the phone. But I didn't think he meant now."

Livvy shivered. "What's going to happen to your house?"

"He said he's found a family to rent it. Until he decides whether I should sell it or not." Books blinked slowly. "Until *he* decides."

Livvy shook her head. "We're freezing, Books. You'd better get inside and decide what you're bringing with you, before he decides that too. Tell him to give me your new address and your phone number."

"I will." Books brought her hands to her face. "Oh, Livvy."

"Go and get warm." Livvy watched her go, watched the slow step, the hesitation on the porch stairs. With everyone moving or dying, and younger families moving in, she and Books had been the oldest in the neighborhood for the last five years or so.

So now Livvy would be the neighborhood grandma. The one who lived alone, whose house was dark at night except for one light. The one asked to baby-sit, sometimes, when no one else could be found. Because teenagers were preferred to take care of babies.

Livvy remembered moving into this neighborhood, with her husband and one daughter and another on the way. Mrs. Johnson had been the neighborhood grandma then. Until she died and left the neighborhood to enjoy its blossoming middle age.

Livvy returned to her house. Her daughter would be calling soon, and she'd forgotten to check the name of the movie the evening before.

The new people were putting up a swing set. Livvy watched through her window as Books's old lawn furniture was pulled into the garage, and a large wooden monster went up. Livvy had seen these things, on playgrounds and such, but never in a backyard. There was a plastic tunnel and a swinging bridge, a bubble you could look through at the top of a tower. She had to look hard to find the swing, but there it was, in between the tunnel and the curly slide. It had a U-shaped plastic seat at the end of a braided chain. Livvy's girls had had odd-sized pieces of wood at the end of ropes.

There was a little girl playing on it now, and Livvy idly watched her as her local daughter's voice swarmed in her ear. She was talking about a movie last night, one about a mother trying to get her daughters back after serving a prison sentence. It was a real-life drama, her daughter said.

The little girl climbed down a rope ladder and stared at Livvy's fence. Livvy watched as she approached the gate and unlatched it. Climbing up, she swung slowly back and forth. Livvy recognized the lidded look, the half-smile. Her own girls had looked like that. She said into the phone, interrupting, "There's a little girl swigging on my gate."

"Oh? From Books's house?"

"Yes." Livvy swayed slowly with the girl's swing. "She reminds me of you. And your sister. You used to love swinging on the gate."

"Do you miss Books a lot, Mom?"

"Well, of course. You don't live next door to somebody for thirty years and not miss them when they go." Livvy glanced into the living room, at the cardboard box next to her chair. Books's son had brought it, said it was full of novels that Books wanted her to have. To keep her company, he said. "Books keeps me company," Livvy had told him. "And I keep company with Books." He had mumbled, shrugged, and shuffled out of her house. Livvy had spoken to Books a couple of times on the phone. It was nice, Books had said, her bedroom, her kitchen, and her bath. But her voice had sounded flat. She'd brightened only when she'd told Livvy about the library that was just downstairs from her apartment. In that building that wasn't a house.

"I worry about you, now. Without Books, I mean." Her daughter was silent for a breath. "That place Books went to is nice, I hear. Maybe you should think about that sort of thing."

"I'm fine, here. I have me to look after. And the house." Livvy searched her memory for the TV listings. Something besides the movie. There'd been a show, that situation comedy, with that comedian. "I thought that show was funny last night. That one with the guy who makes all the jokes." With her daughter's voice droning again in her ear, Livvy walked about making a cup of tea. She looked back outside and saw that the little girl had abandoned the gate and was sitting on her swing, swaying slowly, her feet not leaving the ground.

She was humming. Livvy couldn't hear it, but she could remember.

Livvy was on her porch swing when the little girl came over. She stood by Livvy's side, smiling, her hands clasped. Livvy nodded. "Hello, there," she said.

"Hi. My name is Amber. I'm your new neighbor. Next door."

"Yes, I know. I saw you on your swing."

"And on your gate too, I bet." Amber lowered her eyes. "I saw you at the window. It's okay, isn't it? To swing on the gate?"

"Yes, it's fine, Amber." Livvy smiled. "My name is Livvy. Short for Olivia."

"Hello, Livvy. I was going to have a tea party. Would you like to play too? I'll bring over my tea set. It's new. It's plastic, with blue flowers."

Livvy remembered tea parties with her daughters on this porch. She could bring out the little wicker table from the back room; it hadn't been used in all these years. She nodded at Amber. "Okay. Bring your set. I'll provide the tea and the sandwiches." Amber flew away.

Livvy set the teapot on her stove. Then she made open-faced cucumber and mayonnaise sandwiches, cut into tiny quarters. The wicker table was dusted and pulled to the front. Amber was waiting there, the plastic tea set arranged neatly, when Livvy brought out the refreshments. The little girl watched, eyes stretched open, as Livvy poured the tea into the tiny cups.

"Real tea?" Amber asked.

"Of course." Livvy spooned some sugar into both cups. "And sandwiches, little sandwiches, like they have at real tea parties."

Amber picked up a sandwich and took a small bite. Then she set it back down, neatly, on her plate. "What's on these?"

"Cucumber. And mayonnaise too."

"Oh. I don't like cucumbers." She took a sip of tea, then set it down quickly. She watched as Livvy drank hers and ate two squares of sandwiches.

"I guess I don't like tea, either," Amber said. "It's been nice having this party with you." She left her tea set and ran down the porch steps.

Livvy sat for a while, while her teapot cooled and the sandwiches grew mushy. She remembered now. When she was a little girl and had tea parties with her mother, her mother would squeeze fresh lemonade and serve cookies right out of the oven. With her own little girls, Livvy had made some of that powdered soft drink from the grocery store, the kind with the sugar already added. And sandwich cookies, with white creme inside.

Livvy left the tea set on the table, resolving to wash it later. She collected her purse and set off down the street to the grocery store.

When Livvy pulled the baby portraits from the bottom of her dresser drawer, she was pleased to find that they were still in their frames. She hadn't looked at them for a while, not since she hung up her daughters' wedding pictures. She hadn't remembered storing them in their frames.

She placed the wedding pictures on the floor and hung the babies back in their old places. Standing back and smiling, she remembered each of them. The way the local daughter had cried during her first six months of life. The California daughter playing as she was bathed in the kitchen sink, loving the soap bubbles and hiding her face behind a wet washcloth. The two cribs, two because the girls had been born so close together, and the outstretched bodies of the babies as they slept on opposite sides of the room, one with the covers on, the other with blankets kicked off.

Livvy scooped up the wedding pictures and carried them into the kitchen. There was a proper place for them somewhere in this house, she knew. She'd just have to find it.

The phone rang while she was digging two nails out of her junk drawer. Livvy was tempted to swear when she heard the California daughter's voice. Her list was in the living room; she hadn't been paying much attention to the news this week.

"How are you, Mom?" the daughter asked.

"I've been fine. Busy. Hanging up some pictures."

"Did you buy some new ones?"

"No. I'm just moving your wedding pictures. I hung your baby pictures back up."

The daughter was silent for a moment. "Why, Mom? I thought you liked our wedding pictures."

"Oh, I do, honey. It's just . . . the baby portraits seem more familiar to me. I missed them."

The daughter took a breath. Livvy marveled at hearing her daughter breathe all the way in California. "I hear Books moved."

"Yes. To a retirement community." Livvy rolled the nails in her hand.

"You must be lonely. She'd been your friend for so long."

"Well. There's a new family over there now. They have a little girl. I keep busy."

"A little girl? Mom, don't you think—"

Livvy stood straighter. "Quite a speech the president made the other day, wasn't it?" This was usually safe; the president was always making speeches. Livvy sighed as her daughter launched a political analysis. Then the phone call was over, and California was back on the map and out of her kitchen.

Livvy carried the wedding portraits to the living room. She would hang them by the window, she decided. The nailing was easy, the pictures hung straight. She sat in her chair to admire them.

Noticing the cardboard box from Books, Livvy leaned over and pulled up the lid. She smelled mustiness and sneezed, but reached in and pulled out two books. Then she laughed and hugged them to her chest while she dug out some more.

They were old favorites. Friends. *Gone with the Wind. Green Dolphin Street. The Good Earth.* Books she had giggled and swooned over as a teenager, read behind her mother's back. Livvy caressed the soft, old covers.

Books was right. She'd left Livvy some good company.

Livvy carefully set up the plastic tea set on her wicker table. She could hear Amber's voice crooning from the porch next door. "Amber? Is that you? Come on over," she called.

The little girl came, carrying a doll. Livvy was delighted to recognize Raggedy Ann. She'd had one, and so had each of her girls. "Who's that?" she asked.

"This is Ann, my baby," Amber said. "What are you doing with my tea set?"

"I thought maybe we could have another party. You and me . . . and Ann too." Livvy placed another cup and saucer on the table.

"I don't know, Livvy. Ann doesn't like cucumbers much." Amber sat on a chair.

"No cucumbers, Amber." Livvy opened a package of sandwich cookies and arranged them on a plate. Then she poured red punch and watched Amber smile.

That night, Livvy sat down to read *Green Dolphin Street*. The evening news was over and the television set was turned off. The TV schedule lay opened with the nightly movie circled on it. Hot tea sat at a table by her side, along with a small pile of sandwich cookies. Livvy put her feet up, opened her book, and smiled.

She was comfortable here, in the neighborhood grandma house with the one light on.

sometimes
Robert L. Harrison

Sometimes I remember
my grandmother's hugs
on cold windy days
when the chill of dead
thoughts are buried
deep in my clothing.

Sometimes I think
my grandfather walks
ahead with his smile
hidden by wisps of
smoke fresh from the
forest of dreams.

Sometimes I too smile
as uncles and aunts
appear in a word
or on a fallen leaf
leading me on to a
warmer and safer place.

Sometimes I extend
my hands to hold
them in a circle
and blow out kisses
in the air as they
disappear, one by one.

Photo by Christy Soldatis

the swing
Anne C. Barnhill

Bascom leans in toward the swing, pushes his knotty hands against the bottom board, and shoves gently. The wooden slats need painting, the dark green curls breaking off in his fingers. He sighs and decides he'll get to the task in the fall when the air nips at him with cold, not like the oppressive summer heat that sags in on him today. He's never enjoyed August, the way stillness lies in the atmosphere, heavy and full like the belly of a pregnant dog. He feels the pressure of it in his chest, the difficult breath, the sharp little stings against his ribcage.

He won't think of that now. Instead, he'll keep his eyes on the little one in the swing, his granddaughter, Janey, his Butterball. He notices how her nervous hands have stopped their flight now that she's in the swing, and she's no longer mumbling crazy gibberish to herself. Her clear blue eyes are still vacant, a lost look he can barely stand, but at least she's not slinging her tiny fingers against the air, flailing at whatever she imagines is there.

Swinging always affects her this way. The slow back-and-forth motion calms her like nothing else can. Now, Bascom knows to take her from the womenfolk in the kitchen when he hears their voices go up a notch. He senses Janey's into something, fingers reaching for the brown sugar, tongue licking up spills from the table. And he can tell she needs to step out to the front porch with him, crawl into the swing and fly away from everything.

That's how he likes to think of it—as if he takes her up and up, into the cloudless sky, away from whatever troubles her when she's earthbound. She's only four years old, eighty years younger than he, but her mind's agitated in a way no one understands. He offers her the comfort of air and sky, and though the weather's hot, the movement of the swing cools her a little. He imagines Janey's in a rocket ship, and he's blasting her off to heaven where the hand of God will touch her and her mind will clear the way a foggy mirror does when you press your finger against the glass. He hopes it will work like that someday for his Janey.

She's so tiny, small for her age. Her hair is wavy, the honey color of tall meadow grass in autumn. She has the delicate, dainty features of her mother, Vera, his middle child. Vera has always been his favorite, and she's almost like a shadow of this golden girl seated on the swing in front of him. Vera's hair is black, like his own mother's had been. She's the only one of his three daughters who looks anything like his side of the family. Maybe that's why he's always been partial to Vera. That and her shy manner, so unlike the bossiness of his wife, Estelle, and the other girls.

And Vera is beautiful. He hates to admit it, but her loveliness, the fine-boned face so like his mother's, this, too, causes him to feel a rare closeness to her. And now her tragedy, giving birth to this child who will never be normal, little Janey, this misery confirms Vera in the most special place of his heart.

"Sing, Gwandaddy." Janey's voice startles him. When she speaks, she sounds the way a small bird might, if it could talk. Janey doesn't communicate very often, and she runs over her words so quickly that she's difficult to understand. The womenfolk sometimes lose patience with her, but Bascom doesn't. He knows what it's like to be misunderstood. Fifteen years ago he lost most of his jaw, half his tongue, and all his teeth to cancer. It took a long time for him to make himself clear to people, and he still remembers the barely disguised looks of impatience from Estelle. Even now, he works to shape his words and when he meets a stranger, he must repeat what he says until the new person becomes used to his halting speech.

"Okay, Butterball. How about 'Camptown Racetrack?'" It's one of her favorites.

"Doodah? Sing doodah!" She won't look at him when she talks. Instead, she stares at her hands, which she holds up in front of her face, one hand on top of the other.

He can't manage all the words to the verses so he hums a little, then sings a bit, always careful to say the doodah part at the right time. She joins him. For a few minutes, everything seems normal—a grandfather swinging his grandbaby on the front porch. He wants this moment to last, so he keeps pushing the swing, though his arms start to ache. He's used to the pull, the complaint of tightening muscles, and so he keeps the motion steady and slow. He's developed this technique over the last few months and finds that he lasts longer with the movements calculated and precise.

After a while they fall silent. Both are lost in different worlds, Bascom's the past and Janey's an unknown universe—a dream? Who could know? Bascom recalls when Vera was a girl. It seems such a long time ago now, and he realizes he's smiling at the memory.

Vera caused a stir wherever they went, her raven hair and pale green eyes, the full lips and her sweet expression. Even as a baby, strangers would stop on the street to marvel at her. He'll never forget the old Negro woman who stopped him in downtown Charlotte to tell him that Vera was the prettiest white child she'd ever seen. How he and Estelle had laughed about that, each proud of their girl.

And he remembers Vera calling them late one night in tears, her voice choking over the words.

"There's something wrong with Janey . . . Oh, Daddy . . . " He could swear the phone shook with her sobbing. And there wasn't a thing he could say to comfort her, nothing he could do. The one time she'd turned to him, really needed him, and he was helpless, just an old man marked by disease.

"We'll help, honey. We've got our savings." He'd tried to console her but he knew his words were nothing.

There was silence on the other end of the line, then her husband's voice, explaining that they were doing everything the doctor suggested, there wasn't much they could do anyhow. That was the only time Bascom ever heard Vera cry about Janey. But he knows she keeps her tears hidden, tucks them somewhere deep and private. How he wishes he could wipe them away. What he wouldn't give to fix everything.

He shakes his head, tired out by the dreary thoughts. Janey is watching him, not directly, but with her head down and her eyes cut upward, a sly, sneaky look. She's like a little imp. He's glad she's a normal-looking kid—better than normal. She's cute, though nothing like as pretty as Vera had been. Vera is still lovely, though now her eyes hold a sadness that gives a certain depth to her beauty, a deepening of the spirit that she didn't have before. Sometimes Bascom catches a glimpse of grief as it flashes across her features and she is so beautiful that his heart clinches up in his chest. She's like the paintings he's seen of the Madonna. She has those same sorrowful eyes that seem to know the future and all its heartbreak.

His breathing becomes harder, and he's not sure whether it's from the exertion of pushing Janey or whether it's the usual ball of despair he sometimes feels when he's with the child. He takes a quick glance at his watch, careful not to break his rhythm. Almost noon. He's been at it for nearly two hours. Janey shows no sign of boredom. She never signals for him to stop. He knows she doesn't want to return to this world and he doesn't blame her. He's not crazy about it either.

"Bascom, almost lunch time. You been out here all morning." Estelle's voice is sharp, though he understands that she doesn't mean anything by it. It has become her way.

"I reckon we're about ready, huh Butterball?" The child hums more of their song.

"Janey, go wash your hands and don't forget to use soap. Granddaddy will help you. We fixed a good lunch, so hurry up." Estelle disappears back into the shade of the house, and Bascom pulls the swing to a stop.

"Come on, Butterball, time to eat."

Janey makes no move to get off the swing, so he scoops her into his arms and lifts her down. His big gnarly hand envelopes her tiny one and together they walk into the cool parlor, each silent, each remembering the feel of the swing, the easy flight into the summer air.

first green shoots
Barbara Lockhart

Mary opened the junk drawer in her kitchen and poked through plastic lids, bits of string, and sticky toothpicks, even though at first glance she could tell her paintbrushes weren't there, those long-handled, skimpy-haired wonders as familiar to her as her own hand. She hadn't seen them for a while, though for how long she really couldn't say, and her paints, the yellow ochre and burnt sienna, those tubes sculpted to messy, crinkled forms over the years—they must have a little bit left in them, she told herself as she groped the dark corners of the drawer. In her bedroom she yanked open the nightstand drawer with her collection of hair nets and the eyeglass cases from Dr. Paul Ryland, now deceased, and then pulled open her top dresser drawer with its brown rolls of stockings, scraps of wrapping paper, and crushed bows. Lifting her head to face the wall, she stared through it, thinking.

The dining room hutch.

In the left drawer, she gently pushed aside the graduation photograph of Edna, her daughter, also deceased, and the candle snuffer, stubs of red Christmas candles and crocheted hot pads, a toy train from Luke, her grandson, now grown with a son of his own, and her favorite rhinestone button.

"Cora took them, and the paints too, I betcha," she said out loud, Cora being Luke's live-in girlfriend, like a wife, you know, but not a wife. Not a wife at all. Mary noted the pale green rectangle on the wall surrounded by a sea of smoky green and saw again the painting that once hung there—the white clapboard two-story farmhouse, the chickens that strutted along the fence by the hollyhocks, and the door to the porch kitchen through which she used to find her mother brushing back wisps of grey hair and warming cinnamon toast on the great yellow enameled cookstove.

"I might climb up to the attic today and get them back, put them right where I had them. All my paintings, every one. Gone for—it was spring when they moved in and now the corn's almost ready—five, six months? Shoulda put my foot down right then, at the start," she mumbled. "It's still my house. It's like I've been asleep or something, waiting for them to leave." It seemed important to say this out loud, hands on hips, practicing.

Where was the hand-pump painting? The one with the cornflowers growing around the table where they kept the tin drinking cup. And the chicken painting, with Frank, the rooster, feathers dappled white and black to match his stippled walk as he chased her brothers out of the yard with a fury she hadn't seen since.

"I feel just like that today," she announced to no one.

"What's that, Grandma?" said Luke, coming toward her and scraping his heels on the wood floor. Couldn't he at least pick up his feet when he walked? Him with his bare chest and hair down to his shoulders. Who would have thought men would become more cave-like in this day and age?

And another thing. Besides the paintings, there was the Raggedy Ann doll in the wagon. The one she'd made for Edna when she was four. She hadn't missed it right away, but one night while watching *Jeopardy* on TV, she looked down beside her chair where the wagon had always been and felt as though she were sitting on an island.

Why had she allowed it, this stripping down of her life? Was it because none of them, including her, ever thought she'd outlive this so-called visit of Luke and Cora's? Well, they had another think coming. This old girl was feeling pretty good today. Coming back. She could even see better.

Oh, she didn't mean to seem ungrateful. The rooms she and her Joe had shared in this cottage had grown dark without her knowing it. Darker still when he died eighteen years ago. Until Cora and Luke moved in, she had lived alone with her rag rugs scattered comfortably over the worn spots on the carpeting and overgrown bushes blocking the walk. None of it mattered. She had spent her time filling the walls with her paintings, surrounding herself with the best moments of her life.

She shrugged and looked at the new arrangement of chairs, the bowl of plastic flowers on the TV, the front door flung open and the new curtains billowed out across her armchair. She had forgotten (along with a lot of things) to let the outside air in. And there were new sounds in the house as Kevin, her great-grandson, trampled across the floor and Luke called to him in a singsong voice, "Kevin, Ke-vin. I'm gonna get you, Kevin."

"No, no you're not, Daddy!" His squeals reminded her of Edna. She trembled. Kevin leaned on the seat of her armchair that was just high enough for his elbows to rest on, and peered up at her with the same dark eyes she'd seen in her sleep—like Edna's. "You're old, Great-grandma," he said. Her face must seem like wrinkly old elephant skin to him. She skimmed her fingers over his vernal cheek ever so lightly. A tinge of peach. Maybe yellow ochre and cadmium red light together.

"Yes," she said, then turned her head away. "Luke? Where are my paints? Do you hear me, Luke?"

"Grandma, what you startin' in for all of a sudden? I told you I don't know. Maybe they're with the boxes of things we put in the attic." He had shaved. His chin was wide and strong. It was a good sign.

"Well, I need them. I think I'll be needing them today. Do you hear me? My eyes are better, and the light is good for painting this morning. And while you're up there, you can get my pictures, too, and that Raggedy Ann doll in the wagon. There's even a stretched canvas, I think."

It was useless to ask. He somehow grew up, got opinions about things, and saw himself as boss. An opportunist. Let's go live with Grandma, he probably said to Cora. We'll stay, you know, take care of things—and someday we'll get the house. She didn't begrudge him. He was her only heir. Half Edna. You could see it in his eyes. His best feature. Luminous, they were, and mournful at times. She couldn't deny them anything.

Things might have been different if Edna had not died when Luke was four weeks old. How different everything would have been. Why, *why* was her only child taken? She shouldn't ask, but ask she did, for years—until she just plain got tired of asking. Edna's eyes closed forever as she lay on the stretcher. Mary wasn't supposed to see. The doctor pulled her back and stepped in front of her to shield her from the sight. Blood stiffened Edna's dark, flowing hair. Blood stiffened in Mary's veins as well. Dead still. And Bill, Edna's husband, the driver who had escaped with not even a scratch, held his head in his hands, stiff with fear. It was the drinking, she knew, although he never let on.

The reshuffling after that. The scramble to change everything. Bill married again, and Mary and Joe fled Baltimore to return to Pucum, the gentle, country town of their childhood, like children running home for Band-Aids with hurts too big to heal, while Luke had a new mother, grandmother, aunts and uncles and cousins—Mary only saw him summers on brief visits—he was lost to her, too. Until now.

"Kevin, want to walk to the gas station with Daddy?" Luke asked, pulling his Grateful Dead T-shirt down over his stomach. "Daddy wants to fix the bicycle tire this morning."

Mary tried again. "What are you going to do, Luke? I need my paints, I tell you."

"Thought I'd ride my bike some and strengthen my legs, Grandma. Maybe lose a little of this weight. Besides, the gas tank's low and the check doesn't come for another two weeks."

What would Joe have said? *Get your ass out of here and get a job. It don't look to me like your back is all that bad.*

She would have silently agreed, but she would have defended Luke. Things had not been easy for him. The hands that held him as a baby were different every week, aunts and friends pitching in to care for the infant, who began to scream in terror at the strange faces. She had had her turn, but he only grew worse when she held him because of her trembling. All she could see was Edna with her arms reaching out for the baby she couldn't hold. Mary could not believe in a heaven after that. Edna would surely go to heaven if there was one, but what kind of heaven would it be if you couldn't hold your own baby?

Through it all, Luke had been spoiled. How else could she explain what was happening now? A man who didn't work. A man who lived in his grandmother's house. As a matter of fact, who lived in sin in his grandmother's house. Under the guise of taking care of her.

All those years without Edna and Joe, all she could think about was a family around her. She wanted a kitchen like Mama's, with nine children scrapping and teasing, and bread on the rise on any given day. Steam at the windows. When she was ten she would wipe away the steam and peer out at very nearly the same scene as the one outside her own living room window. The road to Cambridge banked with snow looked the same then as now, even in the cold light of a setting sun. Where did Luke put that painting? The children were sledding along the icy road—last licks before Mama's call for supper. She missed them.

She'd lived too long. This house would have been Luke's by now. Eighty-four. How did that happen? On her last birthday she had called Meredith, the town mortician, about the family plot, and he said he didn't think there was room for her but that he would check.

"Might have to put you in vertically, Miss Mary," he said in his dry, gravelly voice. Mary smiled to herself and wheezed.

"What's so funny, Grandma?'" Luke asked.

"Nothing."

"Want anything from the store?"

"King's syrup and two paintbrushes, a wide one and a thin one."

"Grandma," he drew the word out like he was being *very* patient with her, "they don't have paintbrushes at the IGA."

"No, but Shockley's has 'em. He always keeps a few around for me."

"Now, Grandma. What you want them for? You ain't gonna paint today, and proly not tomorrow neither."

"Either. Yes, I will. I just have to find the paints."

The cookie jar. Could she have put them in the cookie jar? The day Cora and Luke moved in and began cleaning up the place, she had been painting in the kitchen, her easel propped up against the windowsill. She had painted the crepe myrtle in the yard, not that she had a crepe myrtle in the yard but the one at Mama's, where the bush had stood outside the kitchen window, humming with bees in the August heat. Cora had just been saying the paintings in the kitchen had to go. Everything looked lopsided in the paintings, she said as she stood with her feet planted on Mary's kitchen linoleum.

"Maybe after you take some painting classes. They got them at the arts center, where you learn how to draw first? Luke could take you down," she said, with a twitch at the corner of her lips that might have been a smile if she'd let it, her hoop earrings swinging.

Luke let the screen door bang. The loosened screen curled away from the door frame and bounced crazily.

"Luke!" Mary called. "Pick up a yard of screening and some nails for that door, will you?" She heard his boots scrape on the porch, and Kevin say, "Go now!"

"Got some money?" said Luke. "I'd get it but my check won't come for another two weeks." She knew. Lord, she knew. She reached for her black leather bag on the bureau.

Later, in the kitchen, Cora appeared at the threshold with an armful of wet sheets. "How come you don't have a dryer?" she asked.

Mary ignored the question—not all questions were worth answering. What was it she wanted to tell Cora? Oh, yes.

"Did I tell you I had art lessons once?" she said. "There was a Mr. Moss who was teaching classes in Cambridge. He was a very exacting man—painted graphically, like a Disney cartoon, you know? Well, he was trying to get me to tighten up on my style. 'More defining lines,' he said. 'Then fill in the colors. Start with a completed drawing and fill in.' But I just couldn't do it that way."

"You mean like paint the numbers?" Cora could be beautiful. Not every minute, but now, in this minute, with her fleshy arms around the sheets and her eyes that soft green, looking hopeful about everything, looking as though nothing mattered but those sheets if she were to be able to stay in this house. She was just trying to have a home and a family like everybody else on this God's green earth, thought Mary. What binds women together is the nesting urge so deep in our beings.

"What I do is," she said to Cora, because she had never said out loud what it was she did and she thought Cora might understand, "I paint the whole picture together. I mean I keep adding layers while the painting grows. Everything changes as I paint. Big clouds of color like a camera that isn't focused. And then the images come in. Well, sometimes they come in—as if I have to call them from far away."

Cora looked down. She was determined to get the laundry done. She'd chip away at the house and the chores and make a home, and Mary, because she too had a mission this morning, turned and reached for the cookie jar on the shelf above the stove, the silly brown elephant sitting on its haunches and waving its chipped trunk toward her in greeting. She raised the sailor hat lid. Ah, of course. There were the paints, the arthritic tubes, waiting for her like a secret. She left them there and replaced the lid. Now she needed some paper or a board. Canvas would be better, of course, but paper would do. When Edna was little, she painted on paper. Those paintings were gone now, but they were the foundation for what came later. Maybe she had some watercolor paper left. Then she was going to need some gesso so the oil wouldn't bleed through the paper.

The only painting in the house she hadn't done herself was the portrait of Edna that used to hang over the fireplace. She had a picture of her on her prom night that she took to Ella Murphy over in Cambridge. Ella didn't want to paint Edna at first, but Mary told her whatever she did would be fine, that it was impossible for her to do it herself. She had tried, but Edna kept changing on the canvas. She'd turn her head or look down, her nose never looked right, or the space between her lips and nose was too big. She remembered Edna too many ways, or was it that she painted Edna moving through a huge space, from childhood to twenty-one and gone, all in one painting? There was simply too much to tell. Perhaps Edna would have painted. She'd won that prize in high school. She probably would have done things, and Luke would have had good examples to live by instead of an alcoholic father and a disinterested step-mother. Why did Luke put Edna's portrait in the attic, too?

Through the kitchen window, she watched Cora throw the sheets over the line in big bunches and stick a clothespin in the middle of each mound. Somehow Cora had missed a basic or two and didn't know the pleasure of a line of clean, billowing wash on a clear day such as this. Maybe Cora wouldn't mind if she showed her how to hang the sheets properly. Maybe the question really was could Mary stand to see laundry bunched up like that all day. Maybe it was a matter of compromise, and wisdom, and getting along, and deciding what really mattered. Mary didn't know. She had let them have their run of the place. It had been a cold, hard spring. Their coming was like the first green shoots of the daffodils. But it was not like family. It was company that stayed way too long.

"We're worried about you, Grandma, staying alone," Luke had said, like her sisters who had decided five years ago it was time Mary sold the house and went into a nursing home. They talked her into the Methodist House in Federalsburg. One week of hanging her stockings over the footboard of her bed in a chairless room and she walked out. Told them she wasn't ready for playing cards and having nurses checking up on her bowel movements. She took her house off the market and showed up in Mr. Moss's art class, where she began using a dry brush for watercolor. The apple trees along the fence. Sold that one at the art show. Should never have parted with it. The best one she ever did. She knew people in the class shook their heads—that Mary, dabbing with a dry brush, you can't tell her anything. Yet hers was the only one sold.

Holding onto the door frame for that first step, she planted her foot solidly on the cement. Would Joe have an old piece of wood paneling in the shed? He made that doghouse out of paneling not too long ago. Ha! She caught herself. Twenty years ago, at least. Yet it was as if he was still in the shed somewhere, along with the wood scraps he was always using up and saving remnants from, his fingerprints still on the wood, the oil from his hands catching the dust of twenty years. The wood should be ready by now. Ready for her.

"Grandma? You all right?" Cora called. "You want help down them steps?"

"The wash isn't going to dry like that, Cora. You want help hanging it up?"

"Well, if it don't dry, I'll walk it up to the Laundromat."

"I'm all right," Mary said and stepped gingerly down to the walk toward the shed. She felt Cora's eyes on her back.

How many times did she watch Joe's back disappear into the shed? The changes between Baltimore and Pucum bent him. He never stopped grieving as he went about building birdhouses and doghouses to sell. Although he wasn't an old man—fifty-eight was not as old as she had once thought—he had come home to die. She had always been grateful to him for rescuing her from her job at the telephone company and the switchboard at Pucum when everyone thought she was past marrying age. He had whisked her off to Baltimore, and she never once missed the clapboard farmhouse and the noisy clan of brothers and sisters, always believing that she and Joe would produce a crop of kids on their own.

She knew he wouldn't fail her. There was a piece of paneling wide enough and high enough leaning against an old door. She brushed the dust off with the sleeve of her blouse. He always did understand about her painting, when she had to pull into herself like a turtle. Her hand trembled now thinking about him, his red-brown hair, the way he looked at her in the early days. She never forgot.

As she headed for the house, she stopped and leaned the piece of wood against the wash pole. She couldn't help it. Cora was out of sight and she was free to remove the clothespin from one of the sheets on the line and tug at its edges, smoothing it out and lining up the corners so the sheet hung free as a banner to the summer breezes. Before she knew it, all the laundry was assembled like a line of ghosts dancing against the blue sky—Kevin's shorts and Luke's shirts, Cora's nightgown and Mary's housedress. They made a family, didn't they? Shoulder to shoulder, waist to waist?

The walk back to the house was difficult with the piece of wood, and besides, she was tired. Cora met her at the steps.

"What chew want that for, Grandma? We don't need that board in here. Where you gonna put it? Here, lemme take it."

"Now don't you go putting that back, Cora. I've got plans for it. Put it right in my room."

From her bed she could see Luke and Kevin coming up the sidewalk. The fields that lined the road to Cambridge were amber with dried corn. The town, walled in all summer, waited for harvest. She would block out the Agrico grain tower and concentrate on the right blue for the sky, maybe paint Luke and Kevin walking in bright T-shirts and jeans in the lower-left corner. Kevin broke loose from his father's hand and ran toward the house. The screen door banged.

"We got Grandma brushes! But Daddy got no money left for the syrup."

She heard Luke say, "Where is she?"

"In her room with a big board and the cookie jar." Mary envisioned Cora rolling her eyes as she ran her hand through her hair, tossing back her head, her hoop earrings swinging, and Mary grinned to herself, wheezing puffs of air from the back of her throat as she perceived this insistent old thing she had become, sitting on the edge of her bed, still with pictures in her head and none on her walls, waiting for her brushes.

Luke lumbered into her room, the heel of his boot catching on the threshold, the roll of screening tied with string under one arm and a paper bag in the other. Something, something was so familiar about him, yet she couldn't name what it was, only that he drew Edna near.

"You okay, Grandma?"

"My room is bare, Luke."

"No, it isn't! Look at all the junk in here. What's in all those plastic bags, anyhow?"

"Rags for those rugs I make. Leave them be. Luke, I need my paintings."

"We were just trying to clean the place up for you." Innocence and vulnerability, that's what it was. That look about him that struck a chord, moving her beyond his dark hair in sweaty rivers along his neck, the black T-shirt, black boots, and soiled jeans—the uniform of his age—the softness of his paunch at twenty-six, older than Edna now.

She sighed. "Luke, dear, you need to find something of your own to do. Remember the glass etchings you made that summer when you were sixteen? You would sit in Grandpa's shop and sketch roses so beautiful they were ready to pluck. And then you etched them on the glass windows from the old greenhouse."

"I know. I was thinking about it. You can't make any money doing that, though."

"Hmmm." Mary stared past him. Was he going to miss the boat, this child of Edna's? She wished she could say, *Get a job or leave. Marry Cora. For heaven's sake, live right.* That's why old people die off, she told herself. Their ways are as old as they are.

"It's too hot today to get the paintings out of the attic, okay? But I'll fix the screen in the door," he said as if he'd just decided he really should do what she asked, but there was always the chance she would forget and then he wouldn't have to. But maybe sometime he would find work, marry Cora, move on—he didn't know—but not today. *Proly not till the Grateful Dead T-shirt wears out,* Mary thought and began wheezing again at her joke, but stopped suddenly, remembering.

"Luke, I can't imagine why you put away the painting of your mother. At least get that one out for me, please?"

"It's not exactly put away."

"Oh my God, you didn't throw it out, did you?"

"No, nothin' like that. I put it in me and Cora's room."

"Why didn't you tell me, or ask?"

"I was gonna put it in the attic with the others, but it seemed like I ought to look close, study it, you know? Now I can look at her every morning when I wake up. She looks so perfect, like she should have had everything go right, know what I mean?"

"Let me see." It was as if she'd never seen the painting he was talking about.

He put the screening down on the floor with the bag and followed her to his room.

"I hung it careful and all. It's on the wall that don't get sun. You didn't say nothin'—I thought it'd be okay."

It was too easy. Edna all fluffed up in that dress. Like he said, perfect. Not alive. That was how the doctor had put it. He didn't say she was dead. He said, "She's not alive."

"Look," said Luke, "if you want it back in the living room, I'll put it back. Cora don't think much of it being in here anyhow. You okay, Grandma?"

She wondered why they kept asking her. She must look bad. Maybe her bobby pins were falling out. She patted her hair as she walked back to her room. Luke was right behind her.

"Look out," he said. "Don't trip on that screening."

"I see it, I see it. My eyes are good today. You got the brushes in that bag?"

There was a cotton rag in the plastic bag beside her bed soft enough to wipe the piece of paneling clean. Maybe she should dampen it first.

"Would you wet this rag for me, Luke, please, and close the door on your way out?"

The silence in her room was an old friend she had been waiting to see for a long time. She wanted to nest in her memories but also to swoop back and forth through the years with twigs of this and that and make something new.

The paint tubes were stiff but the colors still brilliant. There was enough for a few more paintings. Here was not just blue, but cerulean blue, French ultramarine, and cobalt blue for the sky. She would bring in the corn with cadmium yellow, yellow ochre, and a touch of raw umber and Luke's and Kevin's T-shirts with ivory black, vermilion, and her favorite, burnt sienna.

No, wait. The burnt sienna was for the doll's hair. She would put the doll back in her wagon. No, Edna could put the doll back in her wagon. Her hand would be on the doll, dimpled like Kevin's hand. Kevin could help her. Edna would be wearing her white dress with the blue ribbons. She might turn her head and look like Kevin does, right at her, the same eyes, dark, dark brown, almost black—so black Mary could see herself reflected there. "Look," Mary would say. "Do you see a little girl in my eyes, Edna?" Look quick because little girls grow up. They disappear in a blink. You have to bring them in. You begin dabbing burnt sienna, and who knows, one long buried moment might come back through the mist.

And on that stretch of canvas she'd been saving—it must be in the attic too— she knew then to begin with Edna's eyes. Once she got her eyes, she could even put Luke in her arms and Edna would, at last, be smiling.

acknowledgments

Grateful acknowledgment is made to the following publications which first published some of the material in this book:

A Loving Voice II: A Caregiver's Book, More Read-Aloud Stories for the Elderly (Charles Press Publishers, 1994) for an earlier version of "Possibilities" under the title of "Grandmother Turner's New Life" by Judith Bell; *Fierce with Reality: An Anthology of Literature on Aging* (North Star Press, 1995), *Poets On: Refusing,* Winter 1990, and *Hurricane Alice,* Spring 1998 for "Birthday Check" by Marilyn Boe; *Byline,* No. 198, March 1997, for "Aunt Hattie Visits" under the title "The Butterfly Dress" by Carol Carpenter; *Connections,* 1981, *Only Morning in Her Shoes* (University of Utah, 1990), *la bella figura,* 1992, and *la bella figura anthology* (Malafemmina Press, 1993) for "Knitting" by Barbara Crooker; *Milwaukee Journal* Writing Contest, 1990, for "Thank Heaven for Little Girls" by Ann Elizabeth Dekorsi; *Down on the Corner* (Midwest Villages and Voices, 1987) for "Characters" by Kevin FitzPatrick; *From the Red Eye of Jupiter* (Washington Writers Publishing House, 1990) for "Chewing Thread" by Patricia Garfinkel; *Large Print Literary Review,* Vol. 1, No. 1, July 1997, for "Starboys" by Elissa Goldberg; The Immaculate Conception Photography Gallery (Little Brown, 1994) for "The Damaged Heart" by Katherine Govier; *1995 Festival of Voices Anthology* (Community College of Alleghany County, 1995), *Hemingway's Cafe* (Hemingway's Cafe, 1997), and *Heart Quarterly,* Winter 1998 for "Bread and Roses" by Susan Jacobson; *If Death Were a Woman* (Fox Print, Inc., 1994) for "To My Granddaughter's Future Lover" by Ellen Kort; *Wild Duck Review,* February 1997, for "Her Century" by Scott Lipanovich; *Grit Magazine,* September 10, 1995, for "The Tea Party" by Kathie Lokken; *The Yale Review,* Vol. 78, No. 3, for "The Orange Popsicle" by Catherine Mellett; *Flying Time: Stories & Half-Stories* (Signal Books, 1992) and the 1990 PEN Syndicated Fiction Project for "Sounds" by Elisavietta Ritchie; *Fireweed: Poetry of Western Oregon,* Vol. 3, No. 3, April 1992, for "Bloodlines" by Kelly Sievers; *Swimming into the Light* (NuAge Editions, 1995) for "Photograph of My Grandfather" by Carolyn Marie Souaid; *Along the Path* (Dolphin Publishing, 1997) for "Senior Golfer" by Marilyn Stacy; *Silverfish Review,* Issue 29, for "The Oldest Man in the World" by Michael Strelow; *Passages North* for "Infinity" by Amber Coverdale Sumrall; *Flying Horses, Secret Souls* (Papier-Mache Press, 1997) for "The Truck" by Randeane Tetu; *Ambergris,* Vol. 9, 1993, for "Crayon, 1955" under the title "Gilead, Montana" by Susan Vreeland; *The Panhandler,* No. 23, 1992, for "The Dance Teacher at the Senior Center" by Charles Harper Webb; *Cimarron Review,* No. 106, January 1994, for "The Hundred-Dollar Tip" in a slightly different version under the title "Seagulls" by Ed Weyhing; and *Poetpourri,* Spring 1993, for "Figure of Speech" by Nancy Means Wright.

book discussion guide questions

1. In "Jackie West," by Lisa Vice, we are introduced to a neighbor woman who provides security, comfort, and encouragement to an innocent young girl. As the story progresses, a special relationship develops that will impact the young woman's life. Describe a person or situation you remember as a child who had a profound effect on your world view.

2. In Susan Vreeland's "Crayola," Jenny was introduced to a new world of foreign art and culture, and to new ideas, including guilt and desire. Jenny's curiosity, which led her to snoop through her neighbor's house, reaped great rewards that summer. How did Jenny's grandfather influence her attitude and understanding about her unusual neighbor?

3. Susan Jabcobson helps us understand the importance of compassion in her poem "Bread and Roses." She models a powerful empathy for the woman she is caregiving, but her perception of what is best for her patient changes. How do you relate to her conclusion?

4. Great-aunt Eleanora is a wealth of information, inspiration, and charm in "Sounds," by Elisavietta Ritchie. Where do the sounds come from? In looking forward to your own elderhood, how has this story changed your view of staying home versus going to a home?

5. With humorous and touching clarity, Elissa Goldberg's "Starboys" presents an area of misunderstanding between generations. How did Jack keep his sense of self intact without disturbing his daughter's need to do what she thought what was best for him?

6. Relationships are complex in Rose Hamilton-Gottlieb's "Forgive Us Our Trespasses." Evie's memories of her mother and grandmother enhanced her ability to respond well to her immediate difficulties with her daughter and granddaughter. What did Evie gain from remembering a day when her mother lied about her to a visiting friend?

7. In "The Tea Party," by Kathie Lokken, Livvy learned an important and empowering lesson from the little girl next door. What message did she glean from her new friendship?

8. The taxi driver in Ed Weyhing's story "The Hundred-Dollar Tip," a solid down-to-earth man, seems very grounded in his life. The older man is very light physically and eventually is so light that several huge seagulls can lift him into the air and carry him off. How does this contrast in weight relate to where the two men are on their life journeys?

9. With gentle imagery, Barbara Crooker's poem "Knitting" reflects on the generations of women in her family. Cherished memories are captured within the yarn's final patterns. How would you describe the symbolism in this poem? What symbols would you use to describe your own family members?

contributors

Anne C. Barnhill lives in Kernersville, North Carolina, where she and her husband enjoy their three sons and their three dogs. One of her stories recently won first place in the Porter Fleming Augusta Georgia Arts Council Writing Awards. In 1996, she received a Regional Artist Grant from the Forsyth County Arts Council. She has just finished a novel. p. 176

Judith Bell was awarded a 1997–1998 Individual Artist Fellowship in Fiction from the Virginia Commission for the Arts. Her other awards include the 1989 Washington Prize for Fiction. Her stories have appeared in magazines and journals, including *The American Literary Review, WV Magazine, First for Women, The Washington Review*, and *Snake Nation Review*, and in the anthologies *Grow Old Along with Me—The Best Is Yet to Be* (Papier-Mache Press, 1996), *Farm Wives and Other Iowa Stories* (Mid-Prairie Books, 1995), and *A Loving Voice* (Charles Press Publishers, 1994). She also writes feature articles as an art historian. p. 2

Marilyn J. Boe lives in Bloomington, Minnesota. She has published six chapbooks, and her work appears in numerous publications and anthologies, most recently in *Earth's Daughters, Verve, Sidewalks*, and in Papier-Mache's *There's No Place Like Home for the Holidays*. p. 85

Lori Burkhalter-Lackey was born and educated in Los Angeles, California, completing her photographic training at Otis/Parsons Art Institute. Her photography has been exhibited in many California galleries and has been featured in numerous Papier-Mache books, including *When I Am an Old Woman I Shall Wear Purple* and *If I Had My Life to Live Over I Would Pick More Daisies*. Lori lives in Los Angeles with her husband, David, and their daughter, Annie. pp. 55 and 142

Alexandra Buxbaum began her photojournalism career after attending Columbia College in Chicago. Her work quickly expanded from local publications and small public relation firms to national media such as *Black Star, Agence France-Presse*, the *Christian Science Monitor*, and the *Los Angeles Times*. She is currently undertaking a documentary on the lives of a group of homeless children living at a shelter for women and children. p. xii

Carol Carpenter lives in Livonia, Michigan. Her stories and poems have appeared in or are forthcoming in *Yankee, The Christian Science Monitor, Tampa Tribune Fiction Quarterly, Indiana Review, Quarterly West,* and *Byline.* She received the 1997 Richard Eberhart Prize for Poetry. p. 72

Barbara Crooker has published over six hundred poems in magazines and anthologies, including *Bedside Prayers* (Harper & Row, San Francisco) and *For a Living: The Poetry of Work* (University of Illinois). She has received three Pennsylvania Council on the Arts Fellowships in Literature. She lives with her husband and son (one daughter is in college, one married) and is looking forward to knitting bonnets and booties for the next generation. p. 82

Ruth Daigon was editor of *Poets On:* for twenty years until it ceased publication. She won the 1997 Ann Stanford Poetry Prize and the 1993 Eve of St. Agnes Award. Her poems have been widely published in journals such as *Shenandoah, Negative Capability, Poet & Critic, Kansas Quarterly, Alaska Quarterly, Atlanta Review,* and *Poet Lore.* Her most recent poetry collection is *Between One Future and the Next* (Papier-Mache Press, 1995). Her autobiography appears in the 1997 Contemporary Authors Autobiography Series (Gale Research). p. 1

Ann Elizabeth Dekorsi immigrated to the U.S. from Austria at age six. Currently director of media relations for the Milwaukee School of Engineering and managing editor of its magazine *Dimensions,* she also hosts a weekly radio talk show, "Milwaukee Midweek." In 1990, author James Michener chose "Thank Heaven for Little Girls" as a winner in *The Milwaukee Journal's Wordsmith* writing competition. She's included in *Who's Who of American Women, Who's Who in the Midwest,* and *Who's Who in Media and Communications.* She lives with her husband in Glendale, Wisconsin, and has three daughters and two grandchildren from a first marriage. p. 113

Jeanette Easton lives in Grand Rapids, Michigan, and has always had an interest in photography. Her subjects frequently include her children, Matthew, Allie, Ryann, and Luke; occasionally the family dog, Maddy; and, rarely, her husband, Ken. This is her first publication. p. 33

Betty Sue Fox is a registered nurse with a masters degree in gerontological studies from Miami University, Ohio. Some of her most special friends are from her grandmother's generation. She has published articles in professional journals and poems in various sources. This is her first short story. p. 87

Patricia Garfinkel has published two books of poetry, *Ram's Horn* and *From the Red Eye of Jupiter*, as well as poems in *Seattle Review, Hollins Critic, Pittsburgh Quarterly*, and many other journals. Her new manuscript, *Making the Skeleton Dance*, is currently in search of a publisher. p. 13

Elissa Goldberg lives in Portland, Oregon, where she works as a geriatric social worker. She is a member of Portland's 29th Street Writers and has been writing short stories for ten years. Several of her stories have been published in anthologies and journals. p. 135

Marianne Gontarz is passionate about people, particularly the aging process, which she expresses in both her work and her photographs. Her work has illustrated many books, including *Ourselves Growing Older* (Boston Women's Health Collective), *Growing Old Disgracefully* (Hen Co-op), and Caroline Bird's *Lives of Their Own: The Secrets of Salty Old Women*. A transplanted Bostonian, she now happily resides in San Rafael, California. pp. 20, 43, 79, 84, 86, 108, 112, 134, 155, 165

Katherine Govier, an Edmonton native, has lived in Calgary, Washington, D.C., and London, England, and now lives in Toronto with her husband and two children. She has taught at Ryerson and York University in Toronto and at Leeds University in England. She has published three short story collections and five novels. *Hearts of Flame*, a novel, received the 1992 City of Toronto Book Award. p. 121

Rose Hamilton-Gottlieb's fiction has appeared in *Aethlon, Room of One's Own, The Elephant Ear, Farm Wives and Other Iowa Stories, Prairie Hearts*, and the Papier-Mache Press anthologies, *Grow Along with Me—The Best Is Yet to Be* (1996) and *At Our Core: Women Writing about Power* (1998). p. 143

Robert L. Harrison's poetry has been published in eight anthologies besides his own book, *Green Fields and White Lines* (McFarland & Company). One of his poems was part of *Grow Old Along with Me—The Best Is Yet to Be* (Papier-Mache Press), the audio version of which was nominated for a Grammy. His photography has been on display at Hofstra Law School and Polytechnic University and is in the recent editions of *Animal People* and *Third Rail* magazines (CUNY at Staten Island). He lives in East Meadow, New York, with his wife, Dorothy, and their sons, Roger and Kevin. p. 175

William J. Higginson, poet and translator, is perhaps best known for his work interpreting Japanese haiku and related poetries and chronicling the spread of haiku worldwide in such books as *The Haiku Handbook, The Haiku Seasons*, and *Haiku World*. p. 105

Susan Jacobson actively promotes poetry in her community. In 1997 she was Artist in Education for the Pennsylvania Council on the Arts and the Genera-tions Together Poet for the University of Pittsburgh School of Social Work/ Medical Center. She was Poet in Residence at the Pittsburgh Cancer Institute in 1995 and was founder and peer leader for the Wild Mint and Garlic Writing Workshop in 1994. p. 93

Susan Kan started writing stories four years ago. Some have been published in small journals such as *Mediphors, Hampshire Life,* and *The Berkshire Review.* She makes her home in Shutesbury, Massachusetts, where she works as a copy editor. p. 9

Ellen Kort calls Appleton, Wisconsin, home and names New Zealand, New Mexico, and Colorado her spiritual places of yearning. An author of eleven books, she has received the Pablo Neruda Prize for Poetry. Her work has been performed by the New York City Dance Theater and has been inscribed in stone at the Fox River Mall and the Green Bay Botanical Garden. She teaches poetry and mask making and facilitates writing workshops for domestic abuse survivors and cancer and AIDS patients. p. 153

Jennifer Lagier, cochair of the National Writers Union, Local 7, has published in *When I Am an Old Woman I Shall Wear Purple, If I Had My Life to Live Over I Would Pick More Daisies, Unsettling America: An Anthology of Contemporary Multicultural Poetry,* and *Voices in Italian Americana.* p. 42

Scott Lipanovich has had short stories and essays published in numerous journals, including the *Seattle Review, Abiko Quarterly, Crosscurrents, The Good Life, Gold and Treasure Hunter Magazine,* and *Summerfield Journal.* p. 109

Barbara Lockhart lives on Maryland's Eastern Shore where she writes short stories and works on a novel in progress. She has been published in *Pleiades, The City Paper of Baltimore,* and *Women's Words.* Two of her children's books were published by Tidewater Publishing. p. 180

Kathie Lokken writes and teaches writing classes in Waukesha, Wisconsin. Her short fiction has appeared in *Buffalo Spree, Grit, Passager, Writer's Cramp,* and *Wisconsin.* She has recently completed a novel, *The Color of Bruising,* and a short story collection, *Celebrate!* p. 166

Joyce Lombard is a psychotherapist, artist, and writer. She leads workshops on creativity and spirituality incorporating ritual, and she handcrafts masks and medicine stories about tending images from the collective dream time. A royal blue sea kayak that packs into a suitcase often transports her to the wild heart of place—experiences from which she garners both written and visual work. Coauthor of *Living Creatively with Chronic Illness,* her visual poetry appears in several issues of *Art/Life.* She lives in Ventura, California. p. 96

Katharyn Howd Machan lives, loves, and belly dances (and writes poems about it) in Central New York. As her paternal grandfather, Anton, did with music at the University of Prague and in Akron, Ohio, she also teaches, with words, in the Writing Program at Ithaca College. p. 34

Catherine Mellet's short stories have appeared in literary magazines such as *The Yale Review, Confrontation,* and *Antietam Review.* Her poetry is forthcoming in *Yankee, The Ledge, Visions-International,* and *Poetry Motel.* She is a freelance writer and lives in Ann Arbor, Michigan. p. 44

Susanne E. Moon is the mother of two and the youngest of three sisters. An activities professional specializing in Alzheimer's disease, she is a musician and artist and works with teenagers. Currently working with Molly Fisk, her poetry has been published in *Up Against the Wall, Mother . . . .* She lives with her husband and three dogs in Rhode Island. p. 107

Nancy Moser has published three books of inspirational humor: *Motherhood: A Celebration of Blessings and Blunders; Save Me, I Fell in the Car Pool;* and *Expecting: A Celebration of Waiting and Wonder. The Invitation,* the first novel of her *Mustard Seed* series, came out in April 1998. p. 158

Marilyn Nolt, a resident of Souderton, Pennsylvania, has been providing photo illustrations for periodicals, books, brochures, and calendars for nearly twenty years. Her files include candid images of children and adults as well as landscapes and stills. pp. 12, 70, 156

Elisavietta Ritchie's Flying Time: Stories and Half-Stories contains four PEN Syndicated Fiction winners. Her other books include *Elegy for the Other Woman: New and Selected Terribly Female Poems, Tightening the Circle over Eel Country* (Great Lakes Colleges Association's 1975–1976 New Writer's Award winner), and *Raking the Snow* (Washington Writer's Publishing House 1981–1982 winner). She edited *The Dolphin's Arc: Endangered Creatures of the Sea.* p. 97

Kelly Sievers practices nurse anesthesia in Portland, Oregon, where she has been writing poetry for about ten years. Much of her work focuses on family relationships. *Seattle Review* awarded her the Anna and Perry Lee Long Prize for Poetry, 1997. Her work is forthcoming in *Mediphors: A Literary Journal of the Health Professions,* and her most recent publications are in *Poet Lore, Seattle Review,* and *Prairie Schooner.* p. 80

Sharon Gurman Socol has been a photographic artist since 1977 and has exhibited widely throughout the country. After photographing the 1992 March of the Living, a worldwide program educating Jewish teenagers about the Holocaust and modern Israel, she produced a book and video that combined her photographs with a teenage participant's journal. Recently she incorporated photography and writing in a project to improve self-esteem and literacy with abused and neglected children in Miami. She resides in both Miami and New York. p. 95

Christy Soldatis received her BA from Case Western Reserve University majoring in art history and photography. She photographed for the English magazine *arirang* while living overseas in Seoul, Korea, and continues to photograph in San Antonio, Texas, where she now lives with her husband and two children. p. 174

Carolyn Marie Souaid is the author of *Swimming into the Light* (NuAge Editions), a collection of poems about infertility and international adoption, shortlisted in 1996 for Quebec's prestigious A.M. Klein Prize for Poetry. She lives in Montreal, Canada. p. 35

Marilyn Stacy, a psychotherapist and former college professor, writes both prose and poetry. Her works have appeared in journals, small magazines, the anthologies *Voices from Within* and *Texas Poetry Society*, and a recently published collection of her poems, *Along the Path*. She lives in Dallas, Texas. p. 141

Michael Strelow, raised in Wisconsin, formed his sense of how the world works in the Midwest—lakes, nice dogs, winters that move you to metaphysics. He has lived in Oregon for the past twenty-five years and teaches at Willamette University. p. 71

Amber Coverdale Sumrall has edited or coedited twelve anthologies, including *Storming Heaven's Gate: Spiritual Writings by Women, Catholic Girls,* and *Women of the 14th Moon: Writings on Menopause.* She is codirector of WomenCARE, a women's cancer resource center in Santa Cruz, California. Her collection of poems, *Litany of Wings,* was published in 1998 by Many Names Press. p. 8

Jeffrey Swanberg began seeing life through a lens over twenty-five years ago during a photojournalism class at Northern Illinois University. Since then he has traveled and photographed people and scenes in over twenty countries and throughout the U.S. His photos have appeared on book covers—*The Tenderness of Memory* (Plain View Press, 1994) and *Tonight on This Late Road* (Erie Street Press, 1984)—on calendars (Sports Car Club of America), and in journals. He is director of Student Activities at Rockford Business College. p. 36

Randeane Tetu's stories appear in various magazines, including *The Fiddlehead* and *Massachusetts Review;* in anthologies, including *When I am an Old Woman I Shall Wear Purple;* and in her short story collections, *Flying Horses, Secret Souls* (Papier-Mache Press, 1997) and *Merle's & Marilyn's Mink Ranch* (Papier-Mache Press, 1992). p. 37

Lisa Vice is the author of two novels, *Preacher's Lake* (Dutton, 1998) and *Reckless Driver* (Plume/Penguin, 1996). She grew up in Cicero, Indiana, and lived in Boston, New York City, Main, and California before settling in Thermopolis, Wyoming. p. 14

Susan Vreeland's novel, *What Love Sees,* aired as a CBS movie in 1996. Her stories have appeared in *Calyx, Dominion Review, Alaska Quarterly Review, Crescent Review,* and an essay on her Himalayan experience appeared in *Manoa.* She teaches literature in San Diego. p. 21

Davi Walders is a poet and education consultant in Chevy Chase, Maryland. Her work frequently appears in Ms., literary journals, and anthologies such as *Worlds in Our Words: Contemporary American Women Writers* and two earlier collections from Papier-Mache Press. p. 56

Charles Harper Webb is a rock singer turned psychotherapist and a professor of English at California State University, Long Beach. His book *Reading the Water* won the 1997 Morse Poetry Prize and was published by Northeastern University Press. He edited *Stand Up Poetry: The Anthology* and coedited *Grand Passion: The Poets of Los Angeles.* p. 120

Ed Weyhing was navigator on a U.S. Navy transport ship and president of a computer software company before earning his MFA from Vermont College. Currently he is at work on a novel, *Speaking from the Heart,* and a memoir about his son Paul, who died in 1994. p. 58

Nancy Means Wright has published six books. Her poems have also appeared in various journals, including *Carolina Quarterly* and *Wisconsin Review,* and in anthologies from Beacon Press and St. Martin's Press. A former Bread Loaf Scholar, she lives in New York and in Vermont, where her seven small grandchildren reside. p. 157

more papier-mache press titles
by Sandra Martz

When I Am an Old Woman I Shall Wear Purple
This is the famous book that started the purple craze. *When I Am an Old Woman I Shall Wear Purple*—winner of a 1991 American Booksellers Book of the Year Honors Award—takes a refreshing look at the issues of aging in a society that glorifies youth. Millions of women have taken its message to heart: it's OK to grow older; in fact it's terrific!

"You're not getting older, just a little more purple."—*Milwaukee Journal Sentinel*

ISBN 0-918949-16-5, trade paper, ISBN 0-918949-15-7, hardcover
ISBN 0-918949-84-X, large print

If I Had My Life to Live Over I Would Pick More Daisies
Embraced by readers worldwide, this powerful and insightful companion volume to *When I Am an Old Woman I Shall Wear Purple* illuminates the decisions, public and private, that shape women's lives. Martz once again captures the experiences of women, young and old, as they make the choices that form the tapestry of their lives.

"Some books speak directly to you. And from page one, reading, you think, 'This is me. This could be my life.'" —*Encore Magazine*

ISBN 0-918949-24-6, trade paper, ISBN 0-918949-25-4, hardcover
ISBN 0-918949-84-X, large print

Grow Old Along with Me—The Best Is Yet to Be
A heartwarming collection of writings from women and men exploring the journey through midlife and into old age. These writers transform our myths of aging into a real sense of wonder and expectation. This is the perfect gift both for newlyweds and wedding anniversaries. (The audiocassette version of this book was nominated for a Grammy in 1997.)

"Nothing could be more timely than this book."—Studs Terkel

ISBN 0-918949-86-6, trade paper, ISBN 0-918949-87-4, hardcover
ISBN 0-918949-96-3, large print

papier-mache press

At Papier-Mache Press, it is our goal to identify and successfully present important social issues through enduring works of beauty, grace, and strength. Through our work we hope to encourage empathy, respect, and communication among all people—young and old, male and female.

We appreciate you, our customer, and strive to earn your continued support. We also value the role of the bookseller in achieving our goals. We are especially grateful to the many independent booksellers whose presence ensure a continuing diversity of opinion, information, and literature in our communities. We encourage you to support these bookstores with your patronage.

We offer many beautiful books and gift items. Please ask your local bookstore or gift store which Papier-Mache items they carry. To obtain our complete catalog, mail your request to Papier-Mache Press, 627 Walker Street, Watsonville, CA 95076-4119; call our toll-free number, 800-927-5913; or e-mail your request to papierma@sprynet.com. You can also browse our complete catalog on the web at http://www.ReadersNdex.com/papiermache. To request submission guidelines for our next anthology, write to Papier-Mache Press, 627 Walker Street, Watsonville, CA 95076-4119, or visit our web site.